THE SCIENCE MUSEUM
BOOK OF AMAZING FACTS

MEDICINE

SARAH ANGLISS

ILLUSTRATED BY SEAN LONGCROFT

Hodder
Children's
Books

a division of Hodder Headline plc

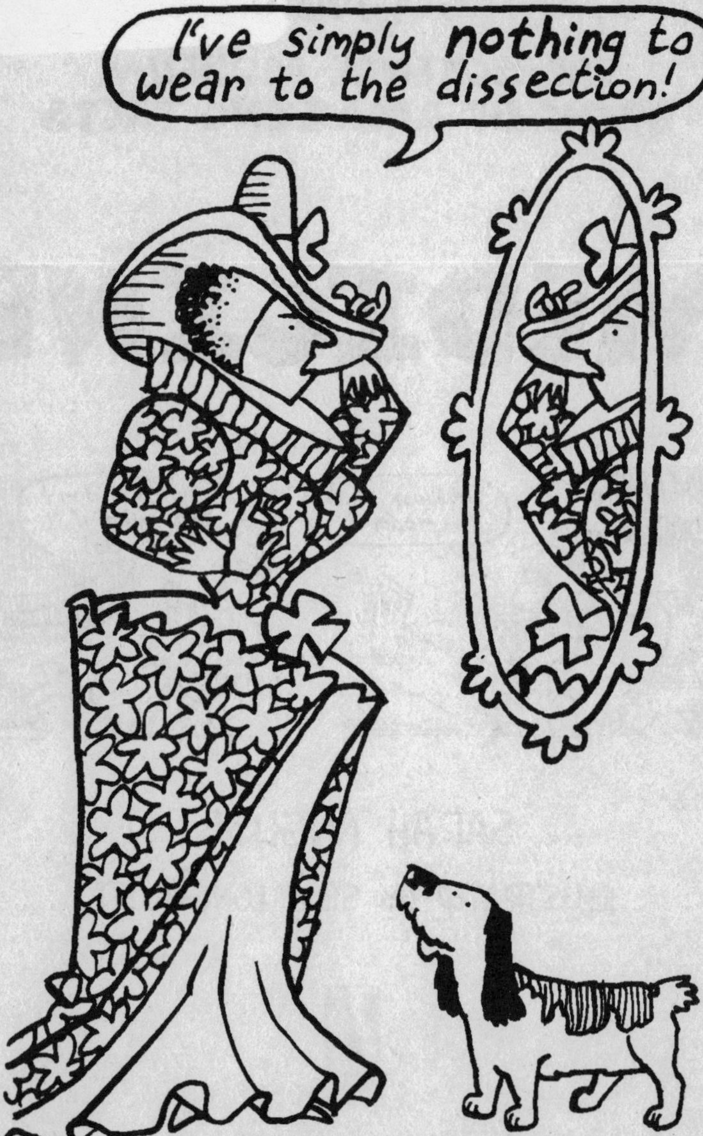
I've simply nothing to wear to the dissection!

sci√m

THE SCIENCE MUSEUM BOOK OF AMAZING FACTS

MEDICINE

Penicillin saved Sarah's life when she was thirteen, so she never takes modern medicine for granted. These days, she tries to stay fit and healthy so she needs to see the doctor as little as possible.
Sarah doesn't smoke and she only drinks a little now and then. Unlike some of her ancestors, she has a bath every morning and cleans her teeth twice a day. When she's not working, she enjoys strolling with a friend who doesn't have a toothbrush and only takes three baths a year – her small Scottish terrier named Bach.

Many of the amazing facts in this book were inspired by exhibits in the SCIENCE MUSEUM in London.
It is home to many of the greatest treasures in the history of science, invention and discovery, and there are also hands-on galleries where you can try things out for yourself.
If you live in the North of England visit the Science Museum's outposts, the National Railway Museum in York and the National Museum of Photography, Film and Television in Bradford.

A Catalogue record for this book is available
from the British Library

ISBN 0 340 71476 X

Designed by Fiona Webb
Cover illustration by Ainslie MacLeod

Hodder Children's Books
A division of Hodder Headline plc
338 Euston Road
London NW1 3BH

Printed and bound in Great Britain by
Mackays of Chatham PLC, Chatham, Kent.

Contents

1 INSIDE STORY	7
Quiz	29
2 AT THE CUTTING EDGE	31
Quiz	58
3 CLEAN LIVING	60
Quiz	74
4 SMALL MIRACLES	76
Quiz	99
5 CAUSES AND CURES	101
Quiz	133
QUIZ ANSWERS	135
INDEX	136

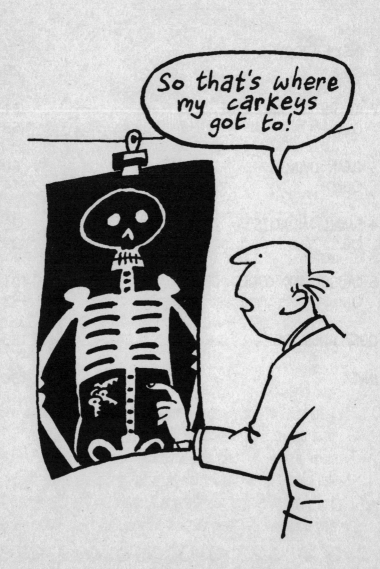

CHAPTER 1

Inside story

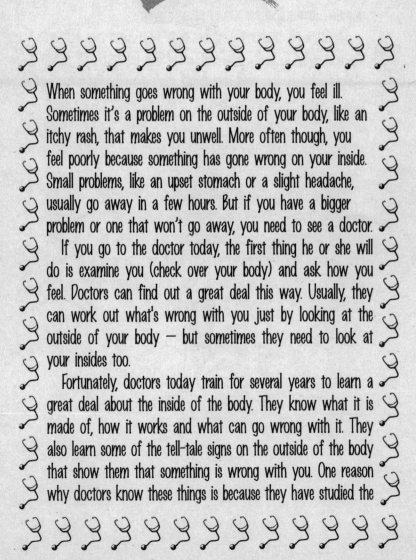

When something goes wrong with your body, you feel ill. Sometimes it's a problem on the outside of your body, like an itchy rash, that makes you unwell. More often though, you feel poorly because something has gone wrong on your inside. Small problems, like an upset stomach or a slight headache, usually go away in a few hours. But if you have a bigger problem or one that won't go away, you need to see a doctor.

If you go to the doctor today, the first thing he or she will do is examine you (check over your body) and ask how you feel. Doctors can find out a great deal this way. Usually, they can work out what's wrong with you just by looking at the outside of your body – but sometimes they need to look at your insides too.

Fortunately, doctors today train for several years to learn a great deal about the inside of the body. They know what it is made of, how it works and what can go wrong with it. They also learn some of the tell-tale signs on the outside of the body that show them that something is wrong with you. One reason why doctors know these things is because they have studied the inside of the human body first-hand. When they were training, they were allowed to study corpses (dead bodies) that had been donated to medical schools in people's wills.

The idea of studying a corpse may not sound nice but it's the best way to really find out about our insides. Until about 600 years ago, this was considered such a nasty thing to do, it was illegal. Doctors had to guess what our insides were made of and how they worked. It was only when doctors could study corpses that they were able to learn much more about us.

Because we have built up so much knowledge over the centuries, doctors today can usually tell what's wrong with you just by examining you on the outside. But if they need to, they can use all sorts of machines to look at the inside of your body too. The X-ray machine is just one of many devices they can use to get a detailed inside picture.

FIRST LOOKS INSIDE THE BODY

MUMMY KNOWS BEST

The Ancient Egyptians had mummies to thank for most of their know-how about the body. Anyone important who died in Egypt 5000 years ago would have been turned into a mummy. Experts in mummifying, called 'embalmers', carried out this work at special temples. When someone died, they removed their brain, liver and other organs, bandaged each part in cloth, bathed them in a specially-made fluid, then put it in its own, labelled pot. The embalmers then wrapped the left-over shell of the body whole.

Now where did I put that pancreas?

Embalmers aimed to stop the body rotting as they believed its owner would need to use it again, organs and all, in a new life beyond death. As these Egyptians rummaged so much around bodies, they had a pretty good idea of what went where – although they could only guess what each part did.

HAVE A HEART

Around 4000 years ago, the Chinese didn't believe clever people were 'brainy' – but they did think they had big hearts. That's because their doctors were convinced that people used their hearts, not their brains, to think. According to them, smart people had bigger and more complex hearts than stupid ones. Unlike the Egyptians, the Chinese didn't think it was right to peek inside the body. That's probably why they relied so much on guesswork. Although they didn't know much about the inside of the body, the Ancient Chinese had great wisdom about curing illnesses and protecting people from sickness (see **It's a wrap** *page 86*). They also knew how to kill pain (see **Pins and needles** *page 50*). To this day, researchers are still trying to fathom out how some of their miraculous treatments work.

TUMMY TROUBLE

Until about 500 years ago, doctors hadn't worked out exactly what the brain and stomach could do. Some of the best doctors in Europe thought that the stomach cooked food. They'd learnt these ideas by reading the books of Galen, a Greek doctor who lived in Ancient Rome. Born about 1900 years ago, Galen was a gifted wound healer. He was often called upon to look after injured gladiators – and to treat the emperor himself. Galen was also a keen and talented researcher. In his spare time, Galen tried to find out more about the inside of the body. Unfortunately though, cutting up human corpses was illegal in Rome, so he could only study the bodies of dead animals. This made it very difficult for him to work out how the human body really worked.

FAST WORK

Imagine how hard it would have been to study dead bodies – human or animal – without a fridge. That's a problem European doctors had to deal with when they were allowed to cut up corpses (dead bodies) for the first time ever. This was around 500 years ago – four centuries before the invention of the freezer.

Before this date, the Christian Church forbade people from peeking inside dead bodies at all. Take the student doctors in Bologna for instance, a city in warm, sunny Italy. They were only allowed to examine two corpses between them all each year. To avoid upsetting any relatives, these bodies had to come from somewhere far away. In warm weather, the bodies' insides were rotten by the time the students could get to them. The students had to work fast to see any important parts before almost everything turned to slop.

EXCUSES, EXCUSES

Even though they'd only had a few glimpses of opened-up corpses, doctors in the 1500s soon began to see ways to improve on Galen's ideas (*see* **Tummy trouble** *page 11*). Until that time, Galen had been top of the reading list for any would-be doctor. Even when some doctors started to realise how the inside of the body differed from Galen's teachings, it was very hard for them to let go of his ideas. After all, many doctors had believed in them for centuries. Some people bent over backwards to defend Galen, even when they found his ideas didn't match what they had seen. The surgeon and teacher Jacob Sylvius, for example, explained that the human body had changed since Galen's times. This, he reasoned, was why Galen's ideas seemed odd. Galen had got his facts right – he was just a little out of date.

CRIMINAL ACT?

A young surgeon named Vesalius was so keen to study the human body, he stole corpses from the gallows pole (the place where criminals were hanged). He smuggled them back to town in fruit baskets and took them back to a secret room where he could open them up, study them and show them off to fellow students. Around 1543, Vesalius drew some wonderful, detailed pictures of the corpses he had seen. His pictures were a great help to other doctors and surgeons for centuries to come. As Vesalius had no time for Galen's books, he became a bitter rival of his former teacher Sylvius, a firm follower of Galen (see **Excuses excuses** page 12). Sylvius thought Vesalius' body snatching was crazy and horrid. Vesalius said that Sylvius was so ignorant about the body, he was a terrible surgeon – the only place he knew how to hold a knife was at the dinner table.

LIFE DRAWING

The great artist Leonardo da Vinci, painter of the mysteriously smiling Mona Lisa, is well-known for his portraits of faces and bodies. But da Vinci wasn't fascinated only by the outside of the body. He became just as famous for his sketches of our insides. Da Vinci, who lived around the same time as Vesalius, also had to steal corpses to carry out his work. He once admitted that he had studied over 100 dead bodies in his lifetime – many of them stolen. Fascinated with everything under the skin, da Vinci drew no less than 779 pictures of opened-up bodies. His best sketches were in such fine detail, they included tiny veins and other body parts that doctors would take another 450 years to fully understand.

SPARE RIB

Until Vesalius stopped to count our bones, many people thought that women had one more rib than men. That's because they had taken the Bible story of Adam and Eve too literally. In *Genesis*, the first book of the Bible, God made the first man and called him Adam. To make sure Adam didn't get lonely, God then took one of Adam's ribs and used it to make Eve, the first woman. People reading this story thought men must be short of a rib. Vesalius didn't just set the record straight on ribs – he also threw out an old myth about teeth. Until Vesalius proved we have equal numbers of gnashers, many people believed that men had more teeth than women.

THAT'S ENTERTAINMENT?

To enjoy a good day out in the 1600s, you may have needed a strong stomach. That's because the place to be seen was the anatomy theatre (the place where dead bodies were opened up). By that time, opening up corpses was far from taboo – in fact it was the height of fashion. The anatomy theatre in Leyden, Italy, for example, had seats for hundreds of spectators. If people couldn't make it to the anatomy theatre, they could always enjoy a public hanging. In those days, many criminals were 'hung, drawn and quartered' in front of large crowds (in other words, after they were killed, they were chopped into four pieces then their insides were pulled out). Student surgeons were often seen taking notes at these grisly events.

STRONG ARM TACTICS

'I see it – but I don't believe it!' This is what the doctor Caspar Hofmann shouted when he was first shown how the heart pumps blood around the body. Hofmann was watching a demonstration by the English scientist William Harvey. It showed the blood pumping through a weightlifter's veins. We now know that Harvey's ideas about circulation were right. But when he first wrote about them in 1628, many doctors thought he was mad. Forty years later, French doctors still urged their King to force others to ignore Harvey. As Harvey knew his ideas might get laughed at, he published them secretly in Germany. Unfortunately, the press that he used made lots of printing errors – so people reading his books thought his theories were even sillier.

DEADLY FEAR

In 1752, a law was passed in Britain forcing murderers' bodies to be given to doctors for study. Around the same time, the American Congress said the same thing must happen to the bodies of people who died in duels (fights to settle arguments). Both these rules were made to scare people into obeying the law – murdering and duelling were illegal.

Many of us today carry organ donor cards (*see* **After you've gone** *page 55*) – we're not at all scared about doctors putting our bodies to good use after we die. But not long ago, people were terrified of the thought of becoming a specimen in an anatomy theatre (*see* **That's entertainment** *page 15*). As almost no one donated their body willingly to medical science, bodies for study were scarce. The number of doctors was growing all the time so the shortage became worse every year. In the 1820s, two of the most notorious criminals in history, William Burke and William Hare, found a ghastly way to end this shortage.

All right – you win... Just promise my body won't be dissected!

GRAVE CONCERN

If a relative died in the Scottish city of Edinburgh in the 1820s, you'd be worried about unwelcome visitors. That's because William Burke and William Hare were at work. Realising there was lots of money to be made from corpses, Burke and Hare used to dig up the dead and sell them to medical students. They stole bodies from graves in Edinburgh then sold them on to a doctor named Robert Knox. He then passed them on to friends in London.

Word about these fiendish 'resurrection men' (men who raised the dead) soon got out. After loved-ones died in Edinburgh, terrified relatives would cover their graves with heavy iron grilles. They hoped this would keep the evil pair at bay. As graves became more difficult to dig up, Burke and Hare decided to look elsewhere for corpses. In 1828, they turned to murder to keep up with the growing demand for the dead.

KEEP OFF THE CORPSE

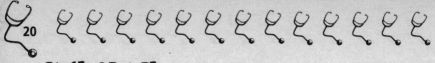

SLICE OF LIFE

These days, you don't have to see a corpse to study the inside of the human body – you can make do with the Internet. The Internet is a global network of computers that lets people share photographs, words and other information around the world.

In 1993, a criminal on Death Row, USA (the place where prisoners condemned to death stay before they are executed) agreed to leave the world a very special parting gift. He gave scientists permission to show his body on the Internet after his death.

In accordance with his last wishes, his body was frozen, sliced like bacon into a million thin pieces, then scanned with a special machine so it could be seen on a computer.

This computer is connected all the time to the Internet. If you have a computer of your own, a modem (a box of tricks that lets you connect with the Internet) and a telephone line, you can connect with this computer and study his body in fine detail from anywhere in the world.

A BETTER PICTURE

HOT SPOT

Before ancient surgeons made the first cut, they sometimes covered their patients with clay. Until inventions like X-ray machines came along (*see* **Hand of fate** *page 24*), there was no safe and easy way to look inside a living body. Even so, thousands of years ago, surgeons in Babylon managed to find out how their patients were under the skin. They realised that sick people were often hot around the part of them that was causing trouble. We now know this happens when the part that's poorly is infected (over-run with unwanted germs). Bodies heat up to try and fight off germs. When surgeons smeared clay on their patient's bodies, they found it often dried quickest over poorly body parts. The drying clay gave them a rough idea where they should do their work.

KEEPING YOUR DISTANCE

The first stethoscope was invented by a doctor who was worried about offending one of his patients. The stethoscope is a set of rubber tubes that goes between a doctor's ears and a patient's body – lots of doctors carry them all

the time. A doctor can press one end of a stethoscope against your body to hear what's going on inside you. Dr René Laennec, inventor of the stethoscope, made the first one out of paper when he needed to listen to a young woman's heart. It was the 1860s and his patient was a Victorian lady. It would have been very rude for him to press his ear against her body – but he knew he had to listen to her heart to find out what was wrong with her.
Remembering a trick he had seen once, he rolled a sheet of paper into a tube and put it between his ear and her chest. To his delight, he could hear her heart beating loudly and clearly through the paper tube – and he wasn't touching her at all!

Young man! – Kindly keep your tube to yourself!

WHAT'S BREWING?

The surgeon Guido Lanfranc used violin strings to check for broken bones. Working over 500 years before the X-ray machine was invented (*see* **Hand of fate** *page 24*), Lanfranc put a string between his patient's teeth and plucked it. The string made the skull vibrate and Lanfranc noticed he could listen to the sound of the string and skull together to find out more about the patient. If Lanfranc heard a dull twang, he knew the patient's skull wasn't vibrating very much. This meant it was fractured. If he heard a sweet note, Lanfranc knew the skull was fine.

300 years later, another doctor, Leopold Auenbrugger, borrowed an idea from his local brewers to check up on patients' chests. Auenbrugger had noticed the way brewers tapped the sides of beer barrels to hear if they were full. He realised he could tap on people's chests in the same way to hear if they were full of muck – a clear sign that they were ill. To this day, doctors still knock on patients' chests to check if they are clear – but if they need to inspect the chest further or look for broken bones, they take an X-ray picture.

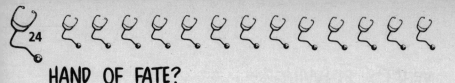

HAND OF FATE?

When people saw the first X-ray image of the body, many of them thought they were seeing a picture of someone beyond the grave. Taken in 1896, this first X-ray image showed the hand of Wilhelm Roentgen's wife (Roentgen was the scientist who discovered X-rays). An X-ray is a form of energy that travels in straight lines, just like light. X-rays can pass through some soft, light materials, including flesh, but are blocked by harder, denser ones, like bone. X-ray images – the pictures of bones that you sometimes see in a hospital – are made by passing X-rays through a body and holding a photographic film behind it. As X-rays can't pass through the bones, the bones block the X-rays, leaving patches on the photographic film that show exactly where the bones lie.

NO PEEKING

As X-rays are quite safe in small doses, an X-ray machine gives doctors a useful way to look at the bones of a living person. Our organs are soft and lightweight, so they hardly block the path of X-rays at all. If doctors want to look at them using X-rays, they usually have to inject them with a dye that will block an X-ray's path. Dyes like these, called 'markers', are often put inside a patient's body to check the workings of their liver, kidneys and other organs. Until the first X-ray machines were built, doctors couldn't peek far into a body without cutting it up. So it's amazing to remember that some doctors who saw the first X-ray machines refused to use them. A few of them insisted that X-rays were no help at all. Others thought they would help them too much – in their opinion, doctors who used them would be cheating.

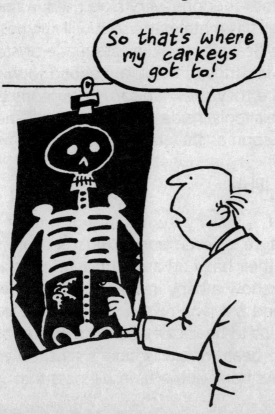

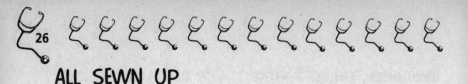

ALL SEWN UP

Many surgeons fear that they'll leave one of their patients with more than they bargained for. During operations, surgeons use lots of scalpels, clips and swabs (small lumps of cloth that mop up fluids). Although everything they use is counted before and after an operation, there's always a slim chance that something will get left behind in a patient's body. Don't lose sleep over this – it hardly ever happens! Just in case it does though, everything used in an operation has metal parts so it will show up on an X-ray. Scalpels and clips are made of steel but special strips of metal are added to swabs to make sure they show up too. If surgeons ever leave their tools inside a patient, they'll spot them as soon as they take an X-ray.

SOUND IDEA

These days, many parents get a picture of their baby before it's even born. That's because they can see their baby on an ultrasound machine. This can show a baby inside its mother's womb. Ultrasound is a type of sound that is far too high for us to hear (see also **Smashing** page 109). If a beam of ultrasound is sent towards someone's body, some of it will pass through their skin and bounce off body parts inside them. An ultrasound machine picks up ultrasound that bounces back and uses it to work out what there is inside someone's body. When a woman is pregnant, ultrasound can be bounced off the baby inside her, completely harmlessly. An ultrasound machine can create a grainy image of her baby on a TV screen.

ATTRACTIVE IMAGE

Although we don't attract pins and paperclips, our bodies are made up of billions of mini magnets. Normally, we don't think of our bodies as magnetic. But the billions of atoms (tiny particles) that make up our bodies act like very weak magnets. When we are near a very strong magnet or are bombarded with powerful radio waves, they spin around. As they are made of different combinations of atoms, different materials in our body spin in different ways. A special ring-shaped machine, called an MRI scanner, makes use of these mini magnets (MRI is short for Magnetic Resonance Imaging). It acts like a very strong, constantly changing, ring-shaped magnet. When we lie inside the ring of the MRI scanner, it measures how it makes our mini magnets spin. A computer uses these measurements to work out how the insides of our body look. MRI scanners can make crystal-clear images of almost anything inside us – from bones and organs to muscles and blood.

Quiz

1   500 years ago, surgeons thought the stomach
    a) covered the brain
    b) made bones
    c) cooked food

2   To get dead bodies that he could study, the surgeon Vesalius used to
    a) buy them from relatives
    b) cut down hanged criminals
    c) poison people

3   People used to think men and women had a different number of
    a) ribs
    b) lungs
    c) teeth

4   To show how blood pumps around the body, William Harvey used
    a) bagpipes
    b) a weightlifter
    c) a rabbit

5   To find out which body parts were making them unwell, some
    doctors used to cover their patients in
    a) clay
    b) steam
    c) blankets

6 Two hundred years ago, American surgeons were given the body of anyone who died
   a) on a train
   b) in a duel
   c) in Pittsburgh

7 The first stethoscope (listening tube) was made to avoid
   a) loosening earwax
   b) being overheard
   c) getting too close to patients

8 Some old graves in Edinburgh have iron grilles to keep out
   a) bodysnatchers
   b) germs
   c) relatives

9 In the past, some doctors refused to use X-rays because they thought
   a) using X-rays would be cheating
   b) X-rays were fake
   c) X-rays would melt the patient

10 In 1993, a criminal on Death Row gave scientists permission to
   a) clone him
   b) infect him with smallpox
   c) slice up his dead body

CHAPTER 2

At the cutting edge

If you ever need to have an operation, you know you'll be in good hands. Surgery today is extremely safe — people don't only go under the surgeon's knife to cure life-threatening illnesses, some even use surgery to improve their looks. What's more, if you are having anything painful done, you'll be given a drug called an 'anaesthetic'. This will make you sleep through the whole thing, blissfully unaware of everything that's happening.

Until about 150 years ago, surgery was altogether different. With no drugs to make patients sleep, the best thing a surgeon could offer was speed. Some operations were so painful, a surgeon had to concentrate on working as swiftly as possible. Surgery must have often seemed a very brutal affair — something that could only be used as a last resort.

Anaesthetics didn't just free a patient from the pain of surgery, they also gave surgeons the chance to improve their techniques. As patients were usually asleep and unable to feel a thing, surgeons didn't have to rush their work. They had the time to work more carefully — and to learn how to carry out complicated and difficult operations.

SCALPELS, SCARS AND STITCHES

NOSE JOB

Centuries ago, you could lose your nose, not your freedom, if you broke the law in India. As noses were chopped off so often, there was a big demand for surgeons who could rebuild them. Amazingly, Hindu surgeons first described how to do this over 2000 years ago. To make a new nose, a surgeon was told to cut a small v-shaped flap of skin from the forehead and pull it down over the face, making sure part of the flap was still fixed to the body. As the flap of skin received plenty of blood, it would slowly grow and fuse into place, making a new nose. As a finishing touch, surgeons were advised to push two polished wooden tubes into the skin to make a pair of nostrils. Italians who went to India in the 1500s learnt how to do nose jobs by reading books written by Hindu surgeons. When they returned to Europe, they made sure their new know-how remained secret. Anyone having a nose job in Italy was kept under lock and key so no one could see how the operation was done.

WONDER WEB

In the 1340s, some French soldiers carried a small supply of spiders' webs. Fighting against the English in the Battle of Crécy, soldiers kept their webs handy to deal with any injuries. They knew if they packed webs into a wound, they would stop it bleeding. The French weren't the only people to heal themselves using insects.

Tribes in India and South America used to clamp termites (giant ants) or beetles around their wounds to hold the skin in place. They encouraged the insects to bite across the two sides of a wound then killed them when their jaws were in place. As the insects died, their jaws gradually tightened around the flesh, 'stitching' the sides of the wound together.

FINE WORK

When boxer Evander Holyfield had his earlobe
bitten off in a match, all was not lost. After he
and his stray earlobe were rushed to hospital,
surgeons were able to sew him back together
again. As well as earlobes, surgeons can sew
back fingers, hands and many other severed
body parts. Looking through microscopes and
magnifying glasses, surgeons are able to
reconnect the arteries and veins, nerves,
tendons (cords that anchor muscles to bones)
and many other fine pieces of a loose body
part. They may need to use hundreds of fine
stitches to completely reattach something that's
been chopped off. If all goes well, a stitched-on
body part can end up in almost perfect working
order. This 'microsurgery' is a long, fiddly job –
but as it can make someone's body whole
again, it's well worth the effort.

LIGHT FANTASTIC

In the past, all surgeons used a knife – but these
days some of them prefer to cut with a laser
beam. A laser is an intense, narrow beam of
light. If it is made powerful enough, it can easily
cut through flesh and other body materials. In

some operations, surgeons find a laser beam works better than a scalpel. As the beam cuts through flesh, it heats it up, sealing the wound and cleaning it in just one stroke. Sometimes, surgeons pass an electric current through the wound to help it fuse together. Many surgeons like to use low-powered laser beams to cut through delicate body parts like the eye. Others use very powerful beams to cut out cancers. Although the surgeon's knife will be here for some time to come, more and more surgeons are learning to work with lasers every year.

SMALL CUTS

No one likes nasty big scars after an operation, so it's good to know that some new types of surgery leave almost no marks at all. That's because surgeons have found a way to operate 'through the keyhole' – in other words through just a few tiny holes in the body. Patients are usually sent to sleep during keyhole surgery, just as they are for an ordinary operation – but as the keyhole surgery uses only tiny cuts, they are given a slightly lighter anaesthetic (*see* **Killing pain** *page 42*).

Keyhole surgeons don't make big cuts through a patient's body. Instead, they make tiny holes that are just big enough to send down a few, thin cables. One cable is a lens connected to a long, thin and bendy cable of plastic. Part of a machine called an 'endoscope', it can get right inside the body and send back pictures of what's there. Another cable is a very fine tube that is used to pump gas inside the patient. This gas blows up the patient's abdomen (tummy) a little, giving surgeons a clearer view of their insides. Other cables carry fine tools that can chop and cut through the body. Surgeons can control these tools from the other end of the cables. After keyhole surgery, patients don't have lots of stitches. Nor do they have to get over a very heavy anaesthetic. This is why they often feel well enough to go home within a few hours.

DOCTORS AND SURGEONS - GOOD AND BAD

SATISFACTION GUARANTEED

If you had money to spend on doctors in Ancient Babylon, you knew you'd be looked after well. After all, the hands were cut off any doctors who killed their patients. In Babylon, doctors didn't come cheap – it cost five gold coins to see one, or two gold coins to send a slave. If you couldn't afford to visit the doctor, you could always take a trip to the marketplace. Sick people would go there and invite passers-by to give them free medical advice.

DOCTORS IN DISGUISE

A pair of doctors who lived 2000 years apart had to wear the same disguise when they worked. That's because they were both women. One of them, Agnodice, lived in Ancient Greece, the other, known as Dr James Barrie, lived in Victorian Britain. Both of them dressed up as men so they could study medicine – something that women in the past were not allowed to do. While she was working, Agnodice was eventually found out to be a woman. Dr James Barrie, on the other hand, kept her secret until her dead body reached the undertakers. Thanks to pioneers like these, we now don't think twice about women wanting to become doctors or surgeons – or men wanting to train as nurses.

COMFORTING WORDS

...And this is from the Queen, -offering you a knighthood!

Violin music, good news and a few friendly words were ordered for patients of Henri de Mondeville. He was one of the first surgeons to stress the need for a good 'bedside manner'. Many of us know it's easier to get better if you feel relaxed and happy. De Mondeville was one of the first people to spell this out to doctors and surgeons. He didn't think you should stop at telling lies if it would help patients get over their illness. He recommended that surgeons should keep each male patient cheery 'with false letters about the deaths of his enemies, or – if he is a spiritual man – by telling him he has been made a bishop.'

HOW CUTTING!

Until a couple of centuries ago, many surgeons weren't thought to be any more skilled than barbers. Pill-giving doctors saw themselves as highly-educated people but considered surgeons to be mere craftsmen and craftswomen (a few women used to work as surgeons too, even though they were prevented from becoming doctors – *see* **Doctors in disguise** *page 37*).

In 1540, British barbers and surgeons were linked together to form a group of workers called the 'barber-surgeons'. This made perfect sense to other doctors who thought surgeons and barbers did a similar sort of job. After all, they both used a knife in their work. These days, both doctors and surgeons are highly respected. People have to train for many years before they can give out medicines – or use the surgeon's knife in major operations.

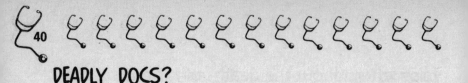

DEADLY DOCS?

When doctors in Los Angeles went on strike in 1976, the daily number of deaths in the city went down. Striking for more pay, the doctors decided to stop all work except emergency treatments. Everyone was terrified that their strike would leave people to die. But they were stunned to find that the number of deaths decreased. Los Angeles doctors aren't the only ones who have this strange effect. When doctors in Brazil downed tools in 1973, the daily deaths dropped by a third. A doctor's strike in Israel that same year cut the daily number of deaths by half. When doctors strike, less people die – but that doesn't mean doctors are deadly. Deaths drop because the most dangerous operations, as well as routine ones, are put off for a while. Sadly, there will always be a few patients who die in dangerous operations.

LIVING DOLL

Between operations, some surgeons 'play' with dolls. They use life-sized, life-like body parts to brush up on their skills. Some even use complete model patients – 'living dolls'. Surgeons can pretend to give one of these model patients an anaesthetic (see **Killing pain** page 42) and check its pulse and blood pressure. They can also try and save it if its pretend-breathing stops – this way they can practise what to do if a person stops breathing in a real-life emergency. Some 'living dolls' are so realistic, surgeons using them feel all the stress and worry they experience in a real operation. Unfortunately, living dolls are specially made so the best ones come with a hefty price tag. Costing over £1 million, they are too pricey for all but the richest hospitals.

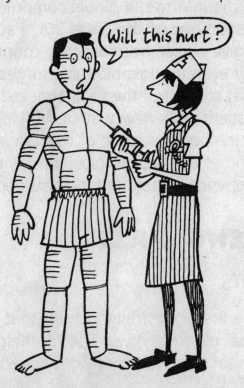

Will this hurt?

CALLING LONG DISTANCE

A surgeon can be in charge of an operation, even though he or she isn't in the same room as the patient. That's because they can watch the operation 'live' on video cameras. If one of the cameras is connected to an endoscope (*see* **Small cuts** *page 35*), the surgeon can see exactly what's going on inside the patient's body. The surgeon can use something like a telephone to tell others who are with the patient what to do. Using the Internet, a global computer network (*see* **Slice of life** *page 20*), a surgeon can even give advice from another country. One day, it may even be possible for a surgeon to use the Internet to control the tools that cut up and stitch a patient. This new way of working, called 'telemedicine', means more of us than ever before can get the best surgical advice, even if we can't physically reach the best surgeons.

KILLING PAIN

COCA NUTS

One of the first anaesthetics (drugs that kill pain or make people sleepy) was used to help surgeons, not patients. It was developed by the

Ancient Incas of Peru over 1000 years ago.
While they worked, Inca surgeons chewed
leaves of the coca plant to calm their nerves.
We now know these leaves contain a powerful
pain-killing drug. Coca has been used through
the centuries to help kill pain. But if you were
unfortunate enough to be operated on in
Ancient Peru, you just had to hope the surgeon
would spit some of the chewed leaves into your
wound.

FEELING NIPPY

A doctor chopping off wounded legs found that
frozen soldiers could hardly feel a thing. The
doctor in question, Dominique-Jean Larrey, was
working in icy conditions around 1810, the time
of the Napoleonic Wars. After one very bloody
battle, Larrey had to amputate no less than 200
soldiers' legs. Remembering what the frozen

soldiers had told him, he packed the legs with ice and snow before he chopped them off. This way, he knew his work would be as painless as possible.

If you have a small operation today – to remove a wart for example – a doctor may numb your pain by spraying you with an extremely cold liquid. Although you'll be fully awake and you'll feel the icy cold spray, the operation itself won't hurt a bit.

FOR WHOM THE BELL TOLLS

The London Hospital still has a bell that was rung 150 years ago to call the terrifying 'holders down'. Unlike operations today, surgery then was a very grisly business. As there were no proper anaesthetics around, even the smallest operation would have been unimaginably painful.

Even if patients knew surgery could save their lives, they would find it very hard to stay still during an operation unless they were forced to. The 'holders down' were strong men who were called in to pin a patient to the operating table while surgery took place.

SPEED KILLS

In one fateful operation of the early 1840s, one surgeon killed three people, including the patient, at one stroke. Before the days of anaesthetics, surgery was so painful, the finest surgeons were the fastest ones. In the 1840s, one of the best surgeons in England was Robert Liston. He boasted that he could amputate (chop off) a limb in less than two and a half minutes. One day, in his eagerness to amputate a leg in record time, he cut off another part of the patient's body and two of his assistant's fingers by mistake. The patient and the assistant died shortly afterwards. But an onlooker was so shocked at this catastrophe, he had a heart attack and dropped down dead on the spot.

WHAT A GAS!

One of the earliest anaesthetics had a peculiar side-effect: it made people dissolve into heaps of giggles. When 'laughing gas' was first discovered, people soon became aware of its merrymaking effect but no one spent much time investigating its use as a pain killer. In 1800, the English scientist Humphry Davy had found out by chance that it could be used to make animals unconscious but others were slow to look into this further. That was until a young shop assistant, Samuel Cooley, went to a popular science talk in the US in 1844. The highlight of this talk was a dangerous demonstration of laughing gas. As the chemist Gardner Colton opened 40 gallons (180 litres) of the stuff, the audience fell into uncontrollable giggles. In the excitement, Cooley badly hurt his leg – but afterwards said he hadn't felt a thing.

PULL THE OTHER ONE

'A new era of tooth pulling!' These were the words shouted by dentist Horace Wells after his troublesome wisdom tooth was pulled out. Wells, who had breathed in some laughing gas, felt no pain at all. He had been keen to try out laughing gas after hearing the story of Cooley's injured leg (see **What a gas** page 45). Wells was so impressed with its effects, he began to use it on his own patients. He then toured America to show off the new anaesthetic. Unfortunately, during a demonstration to some important doctors, Wells gave a patient too little gas. The patient groaned in agony, the doctors groaned in disbelief and laughing gas was given the thumbs down.

POP GOES THE PATIENT

When another early anaesthetic called 'ether' came along, some people were worried that operations really could go with a bang. That's because ether, first used in the 1840s, was highly explosive. There was some concern that it might cause an explosion – maybe inside a patient. One surgeon, William Green Morton, advised others not to use ether at night, when an operation would need to be illuminated by candle light (he was working before the days of electric lighting). Morton was one of the first people to tell the world about ether. A fellow surgeon John Warren was the first to demonstrate an operation using this anaesthetic. After his patient woke up and said he had felt no pain, Warren declared to a crowd of waiting surgeons, 'gentlemen, this is no humbug'.

IT'S A KNOCKOUT

CHLOROFORM – THE WONDER ANAESTHETIC – DON'T MISS TODAY'S GRAND TRIAL!

When James Young Simpson's wife brought him his dinner in 1831, she was surprised to find him and his friends fast asleep.

According to legend, Simpson had invited some fellow doctors over to discuss a new drug: chloroform. A chemist had sent him a bottle of it, recommending it as a safe replacement for ether. Simpson and his party decided the only way to test it was to breathe some of it in. After one of the party opened the bottle, everyone inhaled, became dizzy then fell into a deep sleep. When they awoke, they knew they had found an excellent new anaesthetic.

AGONISING OVER ANAESTHETICS

The first anaesthetics were feared to be so unsafe, some surgeons preferred to manage without them. As the army surgeon John Hall wrote in 1854, 'It is much better to hear a fellow shouting with all his might than to see him sink quietly into his grave.' The anaesthetic chloroform didn't catch on until Queen Victoria used it during the birth of her son Leopold. Extremely pleased by the way it had helped to kill her pain, she wrote in her diary, 'Dr Snow gave me the blessed chloroform and the effect was mild, calming and beautiful beyond bounds.' Once the Queen had used anaesthetics, many more people thought it was all right to use them too.

MIND OVER MATTER

As recently as 1997, a patient went through an entire operation without any anaesthetic. Fortunately, although he was fully awake, he didn't feel a thing. That's because he had been hypnotised, then told that he would not feel any pain. No one is completely sure how hypnotism works. Even so, many have seen the way expert hypnotists can influence what people think. With hypnotism, it really does seem possible for some of us to experience pain-free surgery with no drugs at all.

PINS AND NEEDLES

Believe it or not, Chinese doctors can stop something hurting by sticking needles into you. This therapy, called 'acupuncture' is over 4000 years old. Only experts can carry out acupuncture – they know exactly where to stick their fine needles to kill different types of pain. No one really knows why acupuncture works so well. Some scientists have suggested that the needles block the paths of pain messages that travel along nerves to the brain. Recently, European doctors have tried to build machines that take away pain in a similar way to acupuncture needles. These machines give patients tiny electric shocks along their nerves, blocking pain pathways.

SURGERY'S NEW WEAPON

A drug that was originally an arrow-poison now makes operations safer than ever. Called 'curare', it was brought back from the Americas by the explorer Sir Water Raleigh. When Raleigh showed it to Europeans in 1595, they weren't very impressed. In fact, most people forgot about it until a young Englishman in 1812 started studying its effects on different animals. While some animals were killed by a dart of curare, others survived if they were helped to breathe with bellows. Until curare left its body, an animal would be completely paralysed.

In the 1940s, anaesthetists were looking for a drug that would help keep patient's bodies completely relaxed during major operations. They realised that a form of curare would do the trick. Today, patients are often given a dose of curare during operations and kept alive with a respirator (breathing machine). The curare keeps their muscles relaxed, making it much safer and easier for the surgeon to work.

SPARE PARTS

SELLING YOUR HIND TEETH

If you were young and short of cash 300 years ago, you could always sell your teeth. As the rich ate lots of sugary foods but rarely bothered to clean their teeth, there was always a ready market for young, healthy gnashers. Some people preferred to buy false teeth made of hippopotamus ivory. Others spent their money on 'Waterloo teeth' – teeth that had been extracted from dead soldiers on the battlefield.

Teeth sale! Last few! Everything must go!

HEART IN YOUR MOUTH

The first artificial heart valve may have saved lives but it had one very annoying drawback. It made a loud clicking noise that patients could hear whenever they opened their mouths. A heart valve stops blood flowing in the wrong direction. Made in the 1950s, this artificial one controlled the flow of blood using a tiny plastic ball. As the ball moved back and forth, it made the troubling sound.

Over the last 50 years, people have built many gadgets that can do the work of real human body parts. They have even made machines that can temporarily replace whole human organs, like the kidneys, the heart and the lungs. No matter how good these machines are, they do not work as well as real, living organs. That's why so many surgeons need organs that they can transplant.

YOU'RE NOT MY TYPE

In 1667, a young baron was given blood from a calf. Sadly, this early blood transfusion failed and the man died the next day. The first transfusions rarely worked because doctors didn't know something very important about human blood. It's not safe to give a person any type of blood – only blood from a human with the same 'blood group' will do. Different people have different types of blood and these can be arranged in groups of the same type – these are our 'blood groups'. Until this was discovered in 1901, it was hit and miss whether a transfusion would cure you or kill you. Now, every pint of blood that is donated is screened for disease and marked with its group. This way doctors can get their hands on the right blood when they need it to save a life.

PERFECT FIT

In 1954, a man gave his twin brother a very special gift: one of his kidneys. Our kidneys are organs that clear waste from the blood. Almost everyone has two kidneys but most of us could survive with only one of them. In 1954, a patient of the doctors J. Hartwell Harrison and Joseph Murray was very ill because he had no working kidneys at all. He needed a new kidney urgently – one that was very like his own so his body wouldn't reject it (start to attack it as though it was something that shouldn't be there). Luckily for him, he had an identical twin. This meant he knew someone whose kidneys would be a perfect match for his own. In the first truly successful transplant of its kind, his twin gave him one of his kidneys, saving his life.

AFTER YOU'VE GONE

Did you know that your kidney, liver, heart, lungs, pancreas, intestines, eyes and even your skin and bones could help someone else live after you die? These days, the families of some people who die young get comfort from this fact. They allow doctors to use their loved-one's body to save other people's lives. Many of us now carry organ donor cards to let doctors know straight away that they can use our organs after our death. When someone dies carrying one of these cards, doctors can usually find a welcome home for at least six of their organs, every one of which can improve another person's life.

TISSUE FACTORIES

Imagine how handy it would be if we could grow our own spare parts that perfectly matched our bodies. Amazingly, scientists are already able to grow simple spare parts, like artificial skin. Although this technology is very new, it could be used to give new skin to burns victims or other patients. Scientists have also had a go at making cartilage – the squashy, bendy stuff that cushions our knee and elbow joints. In the end, they hope to grow complete human organs that are a perfect match for individual patients. If this happens, we may never need to carry organ donor cards again.

BREEDING TROUBLE?

Scientists today are breeding animals that have organs which are just right for humans to use. You may not like to think about animals dying to help scientists research medicine or make treatments for the sick, but animals have been used in this way since medicine began (*see* **Tummy trouble** *page 11* and **You're not my type** *page 53*). However, one of the latest uses of animals has upset more people than usual. Using the latest advances in genetics, scientists have been able to breed pigs with some human-like organs. (Genetics is the science of genes – see **Hello Dolly!** *page 97*). There are many people who need a new organ but can't find a human donor. These human-like pig organs, called xenotransplants, could save their lives.

Although xenotransplants offer hope to lots of patients, people have raised lots of worries about them. For instance, is it right to breed animals that have human-like genes? Is there a risk that these animals will spread new, deadly diseases to humans?

Quiz

1   In 1346, a French soldier's first aid kit included a box of
    a) chocolates
    b) ants
    c) spiders' webs

2   When they saw Dr James Barrie's dead body, people were shocked to
    discover he was
    a) a woman
    b) still breathing
    c) on stilts

3   In 1509, surgery was thought to be a similar job to
    a) hairdressing
    b) tax collecting
    c) opera singing

4   One month in 1976, less people than usual died in Los Angeles because
    a) it was very warm
    b) there was a jogging craze
    c) doctors were on strike

5   In 1997, a patient was operated on painlessly without anaesthetic
    because he was:
    a) drunk
    b) hypnotised
    c) dead

6   One of the earliest anaesthetics made people
    a) shrink
    b) laugh
    c) more intelligent

7   Expert Chinese doctors can block pain by
    a) covering patients in ice
    b) chanting special rhymes
    c) sticking needles into patients

8   One of the first-ever blood donors was
    a) an Egyptian Pharaoh
    b) a snake
    c) a calf

9   When people with the first artificial heart valve opened their mouth
    a) they heard a loud clicking sound
    b) the valve fell out
    c) they couldn't breathe

10 The first successful kidney transplant worked because the donor and
    patient were
    a) babies
    b) identical twins
    c) married

CHAPTER 3
Clean living

We take it for granted today that cleanliness keeps germs away. We wash our hands after we go to the toilet, doctors and surgeons 'scrub up' before and after seeing patients, and our towns have clean, well-run water supplies and sewers.

The Ancient Greeks, Romans and Turks valued cleanliness too. They built great bath houses where they could keep clean. Sadly though, as these empires faded, so did the public interest in hygiene. European homes must have been very smelly only 200 years ago as people rarely cleaned their teeth, took a bath or kept their toilet separate from the rest of the house. As water was made dirty with muck from the sewers, smelliness was the least of people's worries. These dirty conditions were ripe for the spread of killer diseases that are carried by water.

Until about 150 years ago, few people understood the connection between germs and disease, so it's not surprising that they didn't bother to keep clean. Surgery and public health improved greatly once people began to accept that germs could cause infections and illnesses. Today, doctors are fully aware of the problems caused by germs. Surgeons even strive to make operating theatres germ-free zones.

GOOD HYGIENE

BY THE BILLION

There are more germs in a single gramme of soil than there are people on the whole of the planet. If you believe it would be healthy to live in a germ-free world, think again. Almost all the germs on Earth live happily alongside us, doing us no harm at all. We could not survive without some germs, like the ones that live in our bodies. We need the right germs in our gut, for example, to break down food. We also need certain germs inside our bodies to fend off other, unwanted ones. Germs only make us ill when our bodies have too many or few of them – or when dangerous ones pay us an unwelcome visit.

KLEENO KLEENO KILLS ALL GERMS!

I hope it, doesn't!

BATH-TIME FUN

If you were a rich citizen of Ancient Rome, Turkey or Greece, the bath was the place to be. Loving nothing more than a good soak, these civilisations sank lots of public funds into building huge bath houses. These were the places to meet friends and relax – as well as get clean. The largest bath houses had several rooms: some with cold water and some with hot. As well as public baths, these people had clean water supplies, unspoilt by sewage from their toilets, that helped their citizens to stay free of many deadly and irritating diseases. The Romans built baths and water supply systems in Britain – but most of them turned to rubble when their empire collapsed. Clean streets, unpolluted water and good toilets didn't reappear widely in Britain until the end of the nineteenth century. They came into fashion because cities wanted to stop the spread of killer diseases like cholera (see **Dirty old town** page 121).

A RIGHT ROYAL STINK

Declaring that she took it 'whether she needed it or no', Queen Elizabeth I had only one bath a month. She lived at a time when few people in

Europe saw the link between cleanliness and
health. Like the rest of her court, she didn't
clean her teeth either. As she ate lots of sugary
sweets, her teeth were yellow, black and full of
holes. They may well have caused her constant
pain. Elizabeth's teeth were in such poor shape,
they sometimes made it hard for her to speak
clearly. Often, she had to cancel meetings
because she had such rotten toothache.

PUBLIC TOILET

Imagine the disgust of an American visiting England when he saw his hosts kept their portable toilet in the dining room. As recently as 200 years ago, even the most wealthy English families didn't keep toilets away from eating places. In rich English homes, the 'close stool' was the height of fashion. This was a fancy, portable box with a toilet inside it.

The American's disgust must have turned to astonishment when his hosts used their close-stool right in front of him, 'deliberately and undisguisedly, as a matter of course' and with 'no interruption of the conversation'.

CLEAN SURGERY

LITTLE MONSTERS

Only 150 years ago, many scientists thought that wasps and beetles came from dung and that mice and frogs were made from slime on river banks. That's because they thought small animals 'spontaneously generated' – popped out of nowhere. Many scientists knew that tiny living creatures, the things we call germs, could be seen under a microscope. But very few of them accepted the idea that germs caused disease. Most of them believed that diseases were spread by a smelly gas called a 'miasma'. Only a few scientists, like the Italian Fracastoro, thought diseases might be spread by some sort of small being.

As early as 1546, Fracastoro suggested 'little creatures' spread diseases. Around 1693, a young man named Anton van Leeuwenhoek saw the 'little creatures' that Fracastoro talked about for the first time. He spotted them under the microscope. Sadly, it took another two centuries for most scientists to accept that 'little creatures' like these could cause disease.

KILLER ON WARD I

If you were in Vienna General Hospital in 1842, a visit from the doctor could be your last. At that time, something in Midwifery Ward 1 was killing one in three women who stayed there. Women who came into the hospital begged to go to a safer ward down the corridor. Four years later, a Hungarian doctor Ignaz Semmelweis decided he should take a close look at Ward 1 to find out what was causing so many deaths. He found that women on the ward were being treated by doctors who had come straight from the mortuary without washing their hands (the mortuary is the place where dead bodies are kept). Through the germs on

MORTUARY

Must dash—
...I'm due in
Ward 1!

their hands, the doctors were spreading diseases from the dead to the living. Semmelweis wasn't thanked when he told hospital chiefs what he had seen. In fact, he was sacked.

A BREATH OF FRESH AIR

Using soap, water, sunlight and fresh air, a team of nurses managed to halve the number of deaths in a wartime hospital. In the Crimean War, hospital conditions were so bad, surgeons didn't even have a place to wash their hands and scalpels between operations. Soldiers, who could wait weeks to get seen, had to lie in dirty beds that were swarming with flies. It's no surprise then that many of them picked up infections that were far more deadly than the injuries that had brought them there. In 1854, a British woman called Florence Nightingale read about these terrible problems and decided to go to the hospital to improve conditions. With a team of 38 nurses, she introduced basic reforms like washing patients with soap and warm water and filling wards with fresh air and sunlight. These simple measures made such a difference, they were later taken up by hospitals back in Britain.

SICKLY SMELL

When a young surgeon heard how the city of Carlisle, England, had dealt with its stinking drains, he found a way to clean up surgery. In the 1860s, Carlisle had suffered a 'big stink' – unbearably smelly drains. The city got rid of the stink by pouring a black sludgy chemical called 'carbolic' down its drains. People didn't know how the carbolic worked but it had killed the germs that were causing the smell. A surgeon, Joseph Lister, noticed that wards full of patients with rotting wounds stank very much like smelly drains. Most doctors thought the stink itself, which they called the 'miasma' (see **Little monsters** *page 65*), made the wounds rot. But Lister thought something altogether different was happening.

CLOUDING OVER

In 1867, Lister carried out a simple experiment that became a milestone in medicine. He filled four glasses with urine, sealed three of them, left them overnight then took another look at them in the morning. The urine in the three sealed glasses hadn't changed but the urine in the open one had gone cloudy. The cloudy sample was bad.

Lister knew that another scientist, Louis Pasteur, had carried out a similar test with alcohol. Pasteur had already shown that alcohol goes bad because of germs. Lister was convinced that germs in the air had caused his cloudy sample of urine to go bad in the same way. Germs could also be making his patients' wounds go rotten.

SMELL OF SUCCESS

Remembering how Carlisle had got rid of its big stink (*see* **Sickly smell** *page 68*), Lister decided to spray patients with carbolic to get rid of germs during operations. This simple measure dropped the death rate after surgery from 1 in 2 to only 1 in 7. Lister had found a way to make surgery much safer. His breakthrough could save countless lives – but sadly, when he first told other surgeons about it, few of them were ready to follow him.

DIRTY WORK

In the 1850s, a Leeds surgeon boasted that he wore the same apron to every one of his operations – without ever washing it! Around that time, surgeons simply rolled up their sleeves and put on their blood-stained aprons before getting down to work. One surgeon, Alexander Mott, used to hold his scalpel and stitching thread is his mouth to keep them handy while he worked. Many surgeons scoffed at Lister when he told them they should disinfect themselves to get rid of germs. In 1877, the surgeon Hughes Bennet taunted Lister with these words about germs: 'Where are all these little beasts? Show them to us and we shall believe in them. Has anyone seen them yet?'

FINAL CUT

If you were unfortunate enough to be a soldier fighting in 1871, the loss of a finger could mean almost certain death. At that time, the Franco-Prussian War was raging – and infections were raging in every military hospital. Of the 13,000 soldiers who had injured body parts removed, 10,000 died. Horrified by the numbers who didn't survive surgery, many doctors decided to try out Lister's new ideas when they returned home after the war. Changing the way they worked was no easy task but they soon found it was worth all the effort. As soon as they took up Lister's disinfecting routine, the number of deaths dropped.

SMOOTH OPERATOR

The first hospital gloves weren't used to stop infection. They were supplied to stop a nurse's hands from feeling sore. People have only been wearing gloves in operations for about 100 years. Worn in 1878, the first surgical gloves were given by American surgeon William Halstead to one of his nurses. Halstead had noticed that the nurse had a rash on her hands.

This rash was made worse by Lister's disinfecting carbolic (*see* **Smell of success** *page* 69). He hoped that rubber gloves would protect her hands from the irritating chemicals. But it soon became clear that the gloves didn't only keep her hands smooth – it also made it harder for her to pass germs between herself and the patient. Before long, people started wearing gloves routinely to help keep germs at bay.

NO TIME FOR TALK

Too much chat is forbidden in a modern operating theatre as talking helps to spread germs. That's just one of the measures that surgeons take to banish germs from the operating theatre. Everyone working in a modern operating theatre must wear specially-made operating gowns, gloves and masks. These are sterilised (boiled to kill germs) or thrown away at the end of every operation. Air is continually sucked out of the theatre and replaced with a clean, fresh supply. Before they are allowed to work in the theatre, staff are sometimes checked out for any nasty germs. Steps like these are all designed to make the theatre a germ-free zone.

Quiz

1 In Ancient Rome, the place to be seen was
a) the public hospital
b) the public baths
c) the public library

2 150 years ago, people thought mice were made from
a) small rats
b) sugar and spice
c) slime

3 In 1842, a doctor in Vienna was sacked for telling his workmates to
a) wash their hands
b) be nice to patients
c) treat the poor

4 The first surgical gloves were made to stop
a) hands from getting sore
b) surgeons dropping scalpels
c) patients spreading germs

5 Once a month, Queen Elizabeth I made sure she
a) ate some sweets
b) had a bath
c) took some exercise

6 Florence Nightingale kept down deaths by making sure wards were
   a) quiet
   b) well lit
   c) clean and airy

7 Used in fashionable dining rooms 200 years ago, the close-stool is a portable
   a) dish washer
   b) toilet
   c) dentist's chair

8 In the 1860s, Carlisle was plagued by
   a) smelly drains
   b) locusts
   c) quack dentists

9 While he was working, the surgeon Alexander Mott used to keep his scalpel
   a) in disinfectant
   b) hidden
   c) between his teeth

10 Operating theatre staff talk as little as possible to cut down on
   a) disturbing the patient
   b) spreading germs
   c) spreading gossip

CHAPTER 4
Small miracles

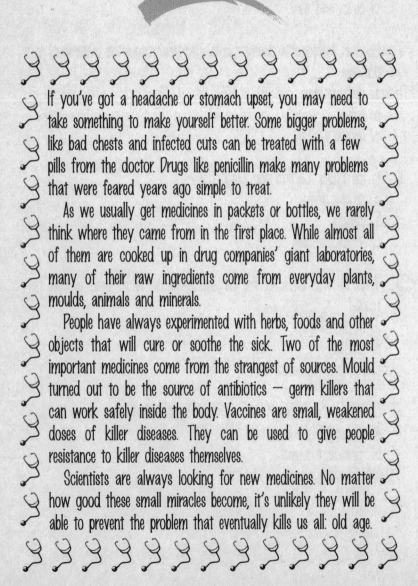

If you've got a headache or stomach upset, you may need to take something to make yourself better. Some bigger problems, like bad chests and infected cuts can be treated with a few pills from the doctor. Drugs like penicillin make many problems that were feared years ago simple to treat.

As we usually get medicines in packets or bottles, we rarely think where they came from in the first place. While almost all of them are cooked up in drug companies' giant laboratories, many of their raw ingredients come from everyday plants, moulds, animals and minerals.

People have always experimented with herbs, foods and other objects that will cure or soothe the sick. Two of the most important medicines come from the strangest of sources. Mould turned out to be the source of antibiotics — germ killers that can work safely inside the body. Vaccines are small, weakened doses of killer diseases. They can be used to give people resistance to killer diseases themselves.

Scientists are always looking for new medicines. No matter how good these small miracles become, it's unlikely they will be able to prevent the problem that eventually kills us all: old age.

ANCIENT REMEDIES

WISE WOMEN

Some of the most gifted healers in mediaeval times were imprisoned and killed as witches. At that time medicine had been banned by the leaders of the early Christian Church, people who had a lot of say over the way countries in Europe were run. They thought God made people sick on purpose – so people had no right to cure disease or kill pain. Although the Church had burned libraries full of ancient cures, they couldn't stop wise people from spreading their herbal remedies and surgical know-how by word of mouth. Some of the only medicine on offer was from local 'sages' (wise women) who knew some traditional and common-sense cures. As very few sages could read or write, they didn't record their remedies. This made Church leaders very suspicious of them. The Church put many thousands of these women to death in terrifying witch-hunts.

TAKING THE WATERS

It's really not a good idea to drink dirty bath water. But in spa towns like Bath and Boston, England, the sick often drank water that had already been bathed in by other sufferers. They believed the spring water in these towns had healing properties. Although they could see they were drinking water that had already been bathed in, they didn't realise this water would make them even sicker. Bathed-in water is usually full of germs so it's no surprise that some ill people felt worse after 'taking the waters' (drinking at a spa). Spa water, raindrops and even the sea itself have all been drunk at one time or another by people seeking cures. The warm, smelly spa water in Bath, for example, has been drunk as a health restorer since Roman times (*see also* **Bath-time fun** *page 62*). Clean spa water does no harm – but it probably doesn't do much good either.

BATH WATER

QUACK ATTACK

Right up until the end of the nineteenth century, quacks (phoney doctors) were still making potions out of ground-up Egyptian mummies, pigs brains, a foul-smelling root called 'devil's dung' and 'unicorns horns'. In 1549, the doctor Ambroise Paré wrote a book that ridiculed these so-called remedies. His book infuriated King Charles IX of France as it made a special mention of an antidote to a poison. This was made of 'bezoar', a stone that forms inside certain animals (see also **Smashing** page 109). Very proud of his own bezoar collection, the King didn't think Paré could possibly be right. But he had to believe him when a criminal who was fed both poison and bezoar died a slow and horrible death.

SWEET IDEA

In the 1600s, newly-weds really did eat honey on their honeymoon. To make sure they had healthy children, they were advised to enjoy a little honey every day of the first month of their marriage. Nicholas Culpepper, a writer who recommended this honeymoon treatment, was one of many herbalists who believed in the healing power of ordinary foods (herbalists were people who made medicines from plants and other everyday things). Six centuries before him, another famous herbalist Hildegard of Bingen wrote detailed notes on the healing powers of everything from trees and plants to crystals and fish. Many herbalists' remedies worked quite well – probably because they were based on a little observation and lots of common sense. For instance, one popular remedy said peppermint could cure stomach ache, another said alcohol could numb pain.

MORE RECENT CURES

DANGEROUS TO KNOW

A scientist who found a substance that could cure some cancers worked with chemicals that were so poisonous, it's dangerous to go near her notebooks even to this day. Marie Curie was the first scientist to discover the existence of a metal called radium. This metal is 'radioactive' – its atoms keep on breaking down, releasing energy and small particles (atoms are the tiny particles that all things are made of). When a fellow scientist Henri Becquerel borrowed a tiny amount of radium from Curie, he was amazed to find it burned his skin through several layers of clothing. This discovery soon alerted people to the possible healing powers of radium. If it could burn through skin and clothing, then maybe it could also burn through cancers. To this day, many cancers are still burned away using carefully controlled doses of radiation.

DEATH BY CHOCOLATE

In the 1920s, you could buy a chocolate bar that was laced with a deadly dose of radium. Called the 'rejuvenator', its manufacturers claimed it would make you feel younger. Ever since people found lots of radium in mines containing the more common metal uranium, they started to search for new uses of this wonder-metal. They knew radium could burn away cancers and they thought it might have life-enhancing properties too. Sadly, they didn't realise that radiation was deadly – even lots of small doses could kill people. The radium toothpastes, hearing aids, skin creams and hair tonics on offer were all pure poison. In the 1920s, some types of paint were laced with radium to make them glow in the dark. As many workers who painted glowing dials on watches started to show signs of deadly cancers, people began to realise that radiation should be handled with care. In 1934, Curie herself died of leukaemia brought on by radium. Sadly, she had been exposed to huge doses of radiation before people had realised how deadly it could be.

GROWING PROBLEM

Could an undiscovered plant hold the key to curing one of the biggest killers on Earth, like heart disease, cancer or AIDS? This is a question that scientists have started to take seriously. For thousands of years, people have used plant extracts to kill pain and make cures. In one way, modern pharmacists (people who make medicines) are not that unlike the herbalists of years ago (see **Sweet idea** *page 79*). Every year that passes, more and more plants become extinct – they can no longer be found anywhere on Earth. Scientists are now worried that we could lose species that we need to make a very important new drug. Such a plant could be a lifeline for humanity. In 1992, many governments around the world took steps to reduce the chances of us losing such a treasure. They promised to help to keep alive as many different species of plants and animals as possible.

MODERN QUACKERY

Quackery isn't completely a thing of the past. In the US alone, 850 million dollars is spent every year on wrinkle creams and other potions that are said to cure the most common problem of all: old age. Although any skin doctor will tell you that these creams never work, they are irresistible to millions who are desperate to banish even the slightest signs of ageing. In the last ten years, people have become interested in the healing powers of crystals and charms. These tokens have no proven medical value – they can't get rid of germs or viruses – but they may help people to feel better. It may be true that people who feel better are able to fight diseases better, using their own body's natural defences.

CLEVER CON

Recently, some Australian medical students were given a skin cream that stopped them feeling the pain of small electric shocks. The fact that the cream worked is even more amazing when you hear it had nothing in it. The cream was an example of a 'placebo' – a dummy drug. Doctors know that you can help some people feel better just by giving them placebos and *pretending* they do some good. Somehow, if you are made to think a drug is stopping pain or making you well, you often get slightly better anyway. Although doctors know the benefits of the 'placebo effect', many of them are wary about giving out placebos. After all, placebos may make someone feel better – which does have some advantages (*see* **Modern quackery** *page 83*) – but they can't get rid of germs or diseases.

VACCINES

WHAT'S YOUR POISON?

A king who lived two thousand years ago used to drink the blood of poisoned ducks. King Mithradates thought this might make him better at coping with any poisons that enemies put in his food or drink. Thinking on the same lines, some African tribes used to eat tiny amounts of snake venom (venom is the poison a snake produces). They hoped this would help them to survive a real bite. Although neither of these schemes really worked, they were very good early attempts at 'immunisation' – protecting someone from a disease or poison by getting their bodies used to a tiny dose of it.

IT'S A WRAP

In India hundreds of years ago, children were regularly wrapped up in the clothes of patients suffering from the deadly disease smallpox. The clothes were full of scabs that had dropped off the people who had this killer. People in India had noticed that children usually picked up a mild dose of smallpox when they were brought in contact with these scabs. If they survived this dose, they would never pick up the full-blown disease in later life. In other words, they became 'immune' to the disease. That's why they wrapped their children in infected clothes.

The Indians weren't the only people who knew how to protect people from smallpox. In Turkey, families protected their families by rubbing smallpox scabs into their arms. In a similar way, the Chinese blew smallpox scabs up noses. Although these measures protected many people from this killer, they did carry a huge risk: about 1 in 30 people who tried them did develop full-blown smallpox and die.

FREEDOM OR DEATH

In 1722, two condemned criminals in Newgate Jail, London, were offered an interesting deal. They were asked to volunteer to have smallpox

scabs scratched into their arms. If they survived and became immune to smallpox, they would be given their freedom. Otherwise, they would be sentenced to death as planned. This test was set up on the advice of Lady Montague, a woman who had seen the way people protected each other from smallpox in Turkey. She was so impressed with the Turks' way of beating smallpox, she had her own children scratched with smallpox scabs. Now she wanted to show her friends back at home how well smallpox scratching protected people from the disease.

DAIRY MAIDS

If smallpox hit your village a couple of hundred years ago, you'd probably wish you were the dairymaid. People had realised for some time that dairymaids never seemed to catch this killer disease. That's because most of them had already caught cowpox – a far less dangerous disease that was passed to humans on cows' udders. In 1774, a young farmer Benjamin Jesty tried to make use of this fact. He took a cowpox scab from a dairymaid and scratched it into the arms of his wife and children. People thought he was very cruel to experiment on his family. They changed their minds, though, when the village was hit by a smallpox epidemic and the Jestys escaped unscathed. From the dairymaid's scabs, Jesty had made the first smallpox vaccine.

ARM TO ARM

Jesty's vaccine worked very well but few people could use it – not everyone knew a dairymaid who could give them some scabs. In 1796, a surgeon Edward Jenner got round this problem by spreading the smallpox vaccine far and wide. First, he took the scabs of one dairymaid and scratched them into the skin of a young boy. When that boy's skin went scabby, he used this to infect other people. Every person's scab could be used to make even more of them, spreading the vaccine in no time at all. Even though it protected people from smallpox, many people were lukewarm about Jenner's vaccine. Some cartoonists showed it turning people into cows. A few priests thought it should be left well alone as smallpox was God's way of keeping down the population.

A KILLER ON DEATH ROW

On 30 June 1999, scientists hope to banish smallpox from the planet altogether. On that day, governments around the world have agreed to destroy the last remaining samples of the disease. In the 1960s, doctors around the world decided to work together to stamp out smallpox. After using the vaccine around the world, they reached their goal in October 1975. Now all that's left of this killer are two tiny, frozen samples that are locked in high-security laboratories in Moscow, Russia, and Atlanta, USA. Although it's nearly time to destroy all that's left of smallpox, some governments are very wary about doing this. What if we could learn more about other diseases by studying these samples of smallpox further? What if we've made a terrible mistake and smallpox is still with us?

THE PARTY'S OFF

There's one millennium party that will have to be postponed. That's the party to celebrate the end of polio. This disease, which paralyses and kills, can be prevented by a vaccine, just like smallpox. Unlike smallpox though, it will still be with us for some time to come. Governments around the world had hoped to get rid of polio by the year 2000, just as they had stamped out smallpox. Sadly, it doesn't look like they're going to reach this target. There are so many wars and upheavals in the world today, many families can't get their children to centres where there are vaccines. Worse still, in some countries, people aren't getting the vaccine at all. As there has been such a breakdown in the vaccination program, the world has a long way to go before it can say goodbye to polio.

MAGIC BULLETS

LOOKING PASTY

Mouldy bread and water used to be a well-known wound ointment in the Ukraine. The people there had noticed this mixture stopped wounds from going rotten. We now know that mouldy bread is a rich source of penicillin, the basis of most modern antibiotics (*see* **What a Dish** *page 93*). It's no surprise then that it worked so well. The Mayan Indians also used an early form of penicillin. They made theirs from roasted corn that they'd left to go mouldy.

Although the people who first used moulds didn't know why they worked, these early penicillins were in use hundreds of years before many history books tell us antibiotics were 'discovered'.

WHAT A DISH

Either I've saved millions of lives ... or I've got some washing-up to do!

Usually, when scientists find their equipment has grown mouldy, they know something has gone wrong. But in September 1928, when Alexander Fleming found mould on the surface of one of his Petri dishes – little jelly-filled dishes that are used to grow germs – he knew he had stumbled on something wonderful. When he gazed at the dish, he was amazed to find the mouldy parts had stopped any germs from growing. After testing it further, he found this mould could be used to kill all sorts of germs without harming the human body at all. We now know he was looking at the raw ingredient of a miracle drug – a magic bullet that could kill germs without harming people. We call this ingredient 'penicillin' and the magic bullets 'antibiotics'.

Antibiotics only work on germs – they cannot kill off viruses at all, like the ones that cause the flu and the common cold. At the moment, many scientists around the world are trying to develop new drugs that can kill viruses. This includes the deadly new virus AIDS (see **AIDS alarm** *page 128*).

TRIAL RUN

Used on 12 February 1941, the first batch of penicillin was so difficult to make, it was said to be more expensive than liquid gold. The person to get this 'magic bullet' was a policeman who was dying from blood poisoning. He perked up as soon as he was given the drug. Howard Florey and Ernst Chain, producers of the first batch, tried to make the drug last by reusing any of it that passed out of the patient's body, for instance in his urine.

We now know people must have penicillin in their bodies for many days before it can kill off unwanted germs completely. Unfortunately, despite all their efforts, Florey and Chain didn't have sufficient quantities of the drug to give the policeman a long enough treatment. Shortly after they ran out of penicillin, the policeman died.

WAR WORK

Penicillin changed war for good – for the first time ever, it allowed almost all war-wounded soldiers to survive. When Florey and Chain first started their work during the Second World War, no one else was interested in it. But as the numbers of wounded soldiers soared, governments fighting the Nazis realised they needed penicillin to stop germs spreading among injured troops. Along with some private companies, they decided to help Florey and Chain find a way to produce large batches of the drug.

By 1943, Florey and Chain only had enough of the drug to treat 100 people. By the end of the war, two years later, they could meet the needs of a whole army.

GERM WARFARE

When they made the first antibiotics, doctors hoped they would protect us from most germs for good. But they soon realised germ-killing is not that simple. The more we use antibiotics, the faster everyday germs change to make themselves resistant to them. Germs can change very quickly because they reproduce very quickly. If we use an antibiotic all the time, over a few years, a germ that used to be killed by it can change into a form that the antibiotic cannot harm. Drug companies have to keep on inventing new strains of antibiotics to keep up with ever-changing germs.

Despite all their work, there are always going to be some infections around that antibiotics cannot treat. That's why doctors have had to think of new ways to make the power of antibiotics last. Many doctors now try to limit how much they use antibiotics – they only use them when they are really needed. They also try to rest certain antibiotics occasionally. They hope the germs will slowly turn into a form that can be caught out by these rested antibiotics in the future.

HELLO DOLLY!

In 1997, a sheep with the strangest family background turned science fiction into science fact. With no father, two mothers and an identical twin that was three years older than her, the animal in question was Dolly, the world's first cloned mammal. As a clone, Dolly has exactly the same genes as one of her mothers. Genes are the packets of information that living things carry in their cells. They help to shape the way things look, grow and act. As she had the same genes as her first mother, Dolly was this sheep's identical twin. Dolly was grown from an egg produced by her second mother. The genes were stripped out of this egg and replaced with those from her first mother. That's how two mothers could be brought together to form one sheep. Some scientists hope to change the genes of a sheep like Dolly so that she can make valuable ingredients for medicines in her milk. They would then like to clone her so they have a whole herd of medicine-making sheep.

Quiz

1 In the 1600s, newly-weds kept themselves healthy by taking regular
   a) spoonfuls of honey
   b) swimming lessons
   c) cold baths

2 In 1996, Dolly hit the headlines because she was the first sheep to be
   a) born with no wool
   b) cloned
   c) crossed with a goat

3 The 'Rejuvenator' chocolate bar was special because it was
   a) fat free
   b) radioactive
   c) an anaesthetic

4 To keep away smallpox, people used to cover themselves in
   a) red petals
   b) infected clothes
   c) blue clay

5 In the 1700s, people noticed smallpox rarely affected
   a) dairy maids
   b) tall people
   c) prisoners

6 On 1 June 1999, governments around the world have agreed to
   a) give everyone a flu jab
   b) destroy the last smallpox sample
   c) cycle to work

7 In the Ukraine, people used to stop wounds from getting infected by
   rubbing them with
   a) brass coins
   b) fried fish
   c) mouldy bread

8 Alexander Fleming found a germ killer when one of his experiments
   a) went mouldy
   b) exploded
   c) was copied by a rival

9 Placebo drugs help some people to feel better, even though they
   a) taste horrible
   b) are poisonous
   c) don't contain any real medicine

10 King Charles IX of France believed in a poison antidote made from
   a) baby's dandruff
   b) stones that form inside animals
   c) toenail clippings

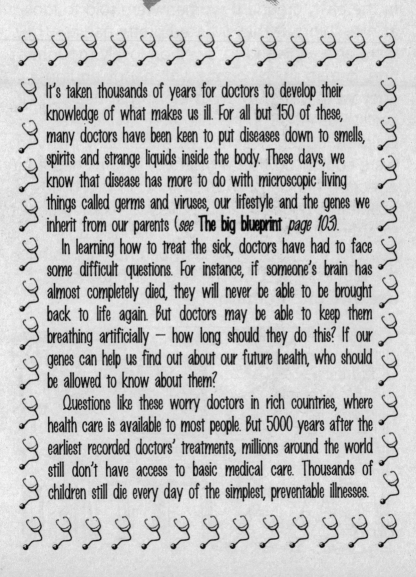

CHAPTER 5
Causes and cures

It's taken thousands of years for doctors to develop their knowledge of what makes us ill. For all but 150 of these, many doctors have been keen to put diseases down to smells, spirits and strange liquids inside the body. These days, we know that disease has more to do with microscopic living things called germs and viruses, our lifestyle and the genes we inherit from our parents (see **The big blueprint** *page 103*).

In learning how to treat the sick, doctors have had to face some difficult questions. For instance, if someone's brain has almost completely died, they will never be able to be brought back to life again. But doctors may be able to keep them breathing artificially — how long should they do this? If our genes can help us find out about our future health, who should be allowed to know about them?

Questions like these worry doctors in rich countries, where health care is available to most people. But 5000 years after the earliest recorded doctors' treatments, millions around the world still don't have access to basic medical care. Thousands of children still die every day of the simplest, preventable illnesses.

CAUSES

LOOKING A PICTURE

In the past, pregnant women were told to look at nice things if they wanted pretty babies. They were also expected to dwell on lovely thoughts and to read slushy books with happy endings. They were urged to avoid looking at bears at all costs. Even though people were aware that children looked like their parents, many of them were convinced that a mother's actions had a big effect on her baby's appearance. In the 1600s, a hospital in Louvain, France was so worried about mothers having ugly babies, it banned ugly doctors. We now know that parents' genes have the biggest effect on the way the baby looks (*see* **The big blueprint** *page 103*).

The apothecary

I demand a second opinion!

THE BIG BLUEPRINT

Around the world, scientists are working on a mission that is bigger than the Apollo program that sent astronauts to the Moon. Called the 'Human Genome Project', its purpose is to find the complete blueprint of human beings (a blueprint is a complete plan for building something). Over 10 billion dollars is being spent on this program to trace and record all the 3 billion chunks of information that are contained in our genes (the packets of information that we inherit from our parents and that we carry around in every cell of our bodies). A single researcher would take 30,000 years to complete this task but scientists are working together to finish the job by the year 2005. As scientists find out more about the human blueprint, they are able to find the causes of some inherited diseases and look for cures.

FUTURE SNOOPING

How would you like it if someone you didn't know could tell how you are likely to die? One day, doctors, employers and insurance companies could get to know an awful lot more about you – even information like this. The way you live your life can have a big effect on your future – but so can your genes (see **The Big blueprint** *page 103*). As scientists learn more about our genes, they may be able to predict more about each of our futures by looking at our individual genes. Who do you think should be allowed to see what they find out?

CURES - GOOD AND BAD

HOME DOCTORS

On the wall of a tomb that's about 3500 years old, there is a message thanking a doctor for healing the Pharaoh's nostrils. The writing on the tomb in Sakkarah, Egypt, is the first anywhere that mentions a doctor curing a patient. Ancient Egypt was full of doctors, many of whom specialised in just one part of the body. Every citizen was a pretty good home doctor too, knowing how to mix up simple medicines. The Egyptians tended to prefer cures that looked like the illness or problem they were meant to treat. They used an ear-shaped plant, for example, to cure ear-ache and a yellow plant to get rid of jaundice (yellowing of the skin). These cures may have looked useful – but they probably didn't do any good at all.

COINING IT IN

In England, hoards of people used to queue up to be touched by the king or queen. They thought the royal touch would cure them of the terrible skin disease 'scrofula'. This cure for scrofula, an illness that was often called 'the King's evil', was most popular during the reign of King Charles II. At allotted times every year, Charles II would lay his hands on sufferers and give them a gold coin. It's likely that many of the people who thought they had scrofula actually had other skin diseases that healed up naturally on their own. That's why so many people thought the King's touch made them better. It's also likely that some people who queued to be touched had nothing wrong with them at all. They went to meet the King because they were keen to get their hands on some cash.

FIT FOR A KING

Not wanting to harm the king, doctors in the French court used to practise their treatments on other people first. In 1686, Louis XIV had a nasty problem with his insides that needed dealing with. Doctors rounded up several people who had a similar trouble and sent them to two different heath resorts. They had no problems finding volunteers – at the time, it was very fashionable to say that you suffered from the same illness as the king. When none of the sufferers showed any signs of improvement after a year's treatment, the doctors decided they would have to resort to surgery to cure the king. No one really knows how well the royal operation went. Afterwards though, the court records show Louis was reluctant to let doctors ever come near him again.

WHAT SUCKERS!

Some poor, sick villagers in Victorian England hoped a cure would be lying in stagnant pools of water. The pools were full of large, jelly-like, bloodsucking grubs called 'leeches'. These days we know it's a very bad idea to drain someone of their blood when they're ill. But the Victorians were following medical advice that had been around since the time of Ancient Greece. Around 400 BC, the Greek doctor Hippocrates said that many illnesses were caused by too much blood (*see* **Big thinker** *page 110*). So when wealthy Victorians fell ill, they would often pay a doctor to apply leeches which would suck away some of their blood. Unable to afford a doctor, many poor people had to make do with wading into leech-infested water.

LIGHT AND AIRY

Open air, good food, sunshine and some gentle exercise used to be the best cure on offer for people suffering from tuberculosis (TB). Right up until the 1960s, doctors in Britain used to prescribe 'sunlight therapy' to people who had this deadly disease. These days, if you're unlucky enough to get TB, doctors will probably cure you with antibiotics (*see* **Magic bullets** *page 92*). In the 1930s though, antibiotic treatments hadn't been developed so sunlight therapy was at its peak. Even when antibiotics were available, doctors would send their patients to 'sanatoria' – special hospitals in the country where they would be given this special treatment. The Swiss Alps and other fresh air resorts had many sanatoria where sufferers would live for weeks. Sunlight therapy worked quite well – partly because it gave poor, working people from squalid cities a chance to enjoy some fresh air and rest.

SMASHING

People with stones in their bodies are finding that treatment is one big blast. That's because the stones can be blasted to pieces with sound waves. When some people's organs don't work properly, or they eat a strange diet, they get tiny lumps of hard materials in their bodies. These lumps, which can be very painful, are called 'stones'. Until recently, doctors could only get rid of problem-stones using surgery. While the patient was under anaesthetic (*see* **Killing pain** *page 42*), their stones were chopped out. Now, they can usually get rid of stones by blasting them with a special type of sound called 'ultrasound' (*see* **Sound idea** *page 26*). This gets rid of them without surgery at all. A very high-powered beam of ultrasound can be pointed towards a stone to break it up. The ultrasound makes the stone shake very fast, turning it into a powder.

BEST OF THE BUNCH

Next time you're ill, it might not be only the doctor who works out how to treat you. Your doctor may use a computer to help decide the best course of action. These days, there are so many different ways to treat illnesses, doctors often have a hard job knowing which ones are best. That's why many of them use computers to help them make up their minds. A special type of computer program called an 'expert system' uses knowledge of other patients' illnesses and treatments to help work out what is wrong with you and weigh up which therapy will suit you the most. If doctors consult this system, it doesn't mean they don't know how to do their job – it simply means they are looking for the best treatment on offer.

WHAT'S UP DOC?

BIG THINKER

One ancient doctor had a greater impact on European medicine than any other. The man in question, Hippocrates, was born in Ancient Greece around 460 BC. Hippocrates was a great surgeon, doctor and teacher. Galen (*see* **Tummy trouble** *page 11*) was one of his many pupils. Hippocrates also wrote many important works on medicine. Some history books say that he wrote 72 books in all but he probably put these together with more than a little help from his friends.

GOOD AND BAD

Hippocrates (and his friends) had an enormous
impact on the way medicine is carried out in
Europe, even to this day. Hippocrates told
doctors to work out what was wrong with

patients by studying their symptoms. This was unusual at the time as many other doctors liked to put diseases down to spirits and gods. He also suggested you could work out what caused a disease by carefully studying lots of people who suffered from it. He warned doctors to keep patients' secrets and urged them to always work to make a patient well. In addition, he gave some useful advice on treating wounds and carrying out simple operations.

Hippocrates put forward some theories about the causes of illness that seem strange to us today. He said the body is made of four different liquids – blood, yellow bile, black bile and mucus – and that diseases occur when we have too much of one liquid and not enough of others.

Hippocrates' teachings had so much influence that blood draining and similar therapies were used in Europe right up until the twentieth century (*see* **What suckers!** *page 107*). His teachings on how to look after patients' welfare are still learnt by student doctors around the world.

TOOTH WORMS

Phoney dentists at the fairground used to pretend to pull worms from people's teeth. Until about 100 years ago, few people thought that germs make our teeth rot (*see* **Little monsters** *page 65*). Many believed that our mouths were full of wriggling worms that burrowed into our teeth, making holes in them. What's more, few people realised that sugary foods rot the teeth.

IN POOR TASTE?

I'll just send this sample for testing, Mrs Jones.

It may not seem nice, but until about 100 years ago, doctors used to taste patients' urine to see what was wrong with them. Doctors had realised that some diseases, like the illness we now call diabetes, made the urine sugary. As no chemical tests had been invented, people could only check urine with their tongues. A medical book written 500 years ago advised doctors to leave this task to their patients or servants as it was 'below the dignity of the physician (doctor) to do it'. Tasting urine made good medical sense. If a doctor today ever suspects a patient has diabetes, he or she is bound to test how much sugar there is in their urine – with a chemical tester of course!

CHEAP TRICK

In the 1440s, a doctor was paid to hold the king's head when he crossed the sea to stop him getting queasy. As kings and queens were dripping with money, they could afford to have many doctors. But until 100 years ago, the poor could never hope to earn enough money to pay for one. A few kind doctors, like John Lettsom, were willing to treat the poor for free. Unfortunately, some rich people took advantage of this offer. In 1840, a doctor reported that some rich patients had borrowed their servants' clothes to visit him. They hoped their simple disguise would fool him into cutting his fees.

REMOTE CONTROL

In the 1350s, doctors treating patients in Plague-hospitals used to shout their instructions from the street (*see also* **Deadly game** *page 126*). At that time there was no cure for this deadly disease so doctors were too frightened to go near their infected patients. Surgeons at that time weren't considered as important at doctors (*see* **How cutting!** *page 39*). They were made to suffer the stench and danger inside the hospital, tending to patients on doctors' behalf. Doctors had only one piece of advice for rich clients who wanted to avoid catching the Plague: 'go fast and go far'. When rich people planned to return after the Plague had left their city, they would often pay a servant to open up their house. If the servant survived this task, they knew it was safe to come home.

IS IT SAFE TO COME BACK IN YET?

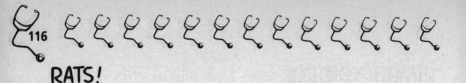

RATS!

People weren't the only creatures that carried
the Plague. The killer disease also travelled on
fleas that lived on rats. For centuries, people
were unaware that rats were Plague carriers.
When Plague-infested ships came into harbour,
people would stop the crew coming ashore but
would take no notice of rats scuttling into town.
The Plague thrived in cities that were full of dirty
streets and wooden houses – ideal homes for
rats. London was ravaged by the Plague in
1663. It is likely the Great Fire of London three
years later helped to get rid of the Plague. The
fire swept through the streets, destroying almost
all of London's wooden buildings in a single
night.

ON THE DEFENSIVE

The risk of getting sued by angry patients has a
big effect on the way some American doctors
treat their patients. People in America are far
more likely to get antibiotics, X-rays, surgery
and other medical care than patients in any
other country. That's not just because they can
afford it – it's also because doctors are terrified
of being sued by American lawyers for failing to
spot an illness or treat it properly. In 1984, a

survey showed that over $15 billion was wasted on unnecessary treatments in America every year. That's probably enough money to cover a small country's entire health budget.

WAKE UP CALL

In the 1790s, loud horns and electric shocks were used to make sure the dead were really dead. At that time, there were lots of horror stories around about people being accidentally buried alive. Very few of them were actually true but that didn't stop people from ordering bells and other devices to be put on their graves. These would enable them to sound the alarm if there had been a terrible mistake. A common way to check if someone was dead was to put a mirror in front of their mouth. The slightest breath would make the mirror go cloudy, telling you the person was still alive.

FLICKING THE SWITCH

Doctors these days can keep people on the brink of death alive. This means they sometimes have to face a very difficult question: are all patients whose heart is beating still living?

Doctors can keep people alive even though their heart and lungs aren't working. They do this by helping them to breathe using a special machine called a respirator. If someone is seriously ill because of an illness or accident, a respirator can be a lifesaver. It can keep a patient breathing until they are well enough to do so on their own again.

Sadly, in some cases, patients can be kept breathing on respirators even though almost none of their brain works any longer. Patients in this state are 'brain dead'. They can no longer think and there is no way they can be made to wake up again. In these cases, families, doctors and even judges have to help make the difficult decision about whether to turn off the respirator.

MODERN MUMMIES

Some rich and hopeful people have had their bodies frozen after their death. They hope that doctors in the future will be able to thaw them out, bring them back to life, then cure them of any diseases that killed them in the first place.

Although some people spend their life-savings on 'cryonic suspension' – storage in a very cold deep freeze – it's unlikely they will ever get value for money. Cryonic centres faithfully monitor their 'customers' and make sure their temperature never gets too high. However, in the end, it's unlikely doctors will ever be able to revive them. As the liquids in their bodies froze, they expanded and damaged their cells.

People who believe in cryonics are not put off by this fact. Some are convinced that tiny 'nanomachines' (machines that are just a millionth of a millimetre in size) will be able to scuttle around their bodies, repairing any damage. In cryonics, only one thing is certain: dissatisfied customers will never ask for their money back.

PREVENTION BETTER THAN CURE

GETTING COLD FEET

Many loving parents of the 1760s plunged their children into ice-cold water every morning. They thought a freezing dip would help their little

darlings ward off colds, flu and other diseases.
For good measure, some well-meaning wealthy
families only allowed their children to have
shoes with thin soles – at a time when poorer
children couldn't afford any shoes at all. These
wealthy people thought their children would
grow up tougher if they were used to feeling
chilly. That's why they wanted their feet to be
cold and wet. Even the great scientist Benjamin
Franklin enjoyed the craze for being icy. Firmly
believing that a daily dose of cold air made him
stronger, he wrote, 'I rise every morning and sit
in my chamber without any clothes whatever,
half an hour to an hour according to the
season, whether reading or writing.'

DIRTY OLD TOWN

If you took water from a certain London pump
in 1854, that drink could be your last. At the
time, London was in the grip of a deadly
cholera epidemic. Cholera is a killer disease
spread by germs that live in dirty water. In the
1850s, no one knew its cause. Many people
thought it was spread by stinking air or the
stench of old Plague pits (graves where lots of
Plague victims were buried together) – but a
few doctors thought it might be spread by

something nasty in the water. One of those doctors was John Snow. He'd noticed that cholera struck most often in overcrowded homes that had no proper toilets.

POISONED PUMP

Armed with nothing but common sense, John Snow managed to beat the cholera bug. He'd noticed that the epidemic had killed no less than 344 people, all of whom lived within a few streets of each other. After talking to the relatives of the victims, he found they had all drunk water from the same pump, one in Broad Street.

Snow decided to study maps of underground London to find out where the water from this pump came from. All of it came from the Thames – but some was fed from a pipe that was just a few hundred metres downstream from a huge sewage outlet. As soon as he realised this, Snow ordered the pump handle at Broad Street to be removed. Within weeks, the epidemic was over.

THE BIG KILLERS

GIVEN HALF A CHANCE

A single disease, malaria, has killed half the people who ever lived on Earth. Malaria, which means 'bad air', is a *parasite* (a tiny creature that can only live in or on another living thing), carried by a certain type of mosquito (a fly-like insect that breeds over ponds in hot, moist areas). If one of these mosquitoes bites you, malaria can pass into your bloodstream. In the 1880s, scientists realised for the first time that mosquitoes carry malaria. They started to spray ponds with oil to stop the insects from hatching. This century, they have replaced ordinary oil with a powerful pesticide (insect killer) called DDT. This has caused a serious, unexpected problem: a new type of mosquito has evolved that cannot be killed by DDT.

TYPHOID MARY

Until she was stopped by health officials, travelling cook Mary Mallon unknowingly spread disease and death wherever she went. Living at the beginning of this century, Mallon was infected with the deadly disease typhoid but never got the symptoms of it herself. Unaware of the killer she carried, she continued working, passing on typhoid germs to the customers she cooked and prepared food for. Within a few weeks, over 53 of her customers were taken ill. Five of them died. Mallon's customers spread her germs further, eventually making over 1300 people ill. Health officials finally tracked 'Typhoid Mary' down in a top-notch hotel in Park Lane, New York. Once caught, the unfortunate cook was forbidden ever to work again.

KILLER WEED

Today, we all know that smoking kills – in the UK, it causes more deaths than road accidents, drug abuse, murder, suicide and AIDS put together. In the past though, some companies tried to sell tobacco as a health restorer. In 1742, an advert in the *London Daily Advertiser* declared that smoking was 'good for the head, eyes, lungs, rheumatism, gout, thickness of

hearing, head-ache, tooth-ache, vapours, etc.'
Believe it or not, a few cigarette companies tried
to pretend smoking was good for you right up
until the 1950s.

DEADLY GAME

Ring a ring of roses
A pocket full of posies
Atishoo! Atishoo!
We all fall down.

If you enjoyed saying this nursery rhyme when you were little, you may be surprised to know it could be about one of the deadliest diseases of all time: the Plague. Also known as the Black Death, the Plague swept around the world in several waves of global epidemics between 1380 and 1700. It killed 32 million people, a third of the world's population over that period. People with the Plague have an area of dark blotches on their skin: *a ring of roses*. There has only been a vaccine for the Plague since 1895 (*see* **Vaccines** *page 86*). Centuries before that, people thought they could protect themselves from it by sniffing *posies* – bunches of fresh flowers. If you got the Plague, you were bound to *fall down* dead within days.

DOWN THE DRAIN

In 1948, a team of scientists managed to track down a typhoid sufferer by looking through the local drains. They knew the deadly disease was in town but they couldn't work out where it was coming from. They also realised that anyone who had typhoid germs would flush them into the sewer every time they used the toilet. The scientists looked for the germs in different parts of the sewers. From these, they were able to work out which branch of the sewer the typhoid-infected sewage had come from. Eventually, they traced the toilet that the person carrying the disease had just been using. To this day, scientists regularly check for the disease in the sewers. They constantly monitor sewage to make sure no new ones are developing.

At last! – I think we've found it!

AIDS ALARM

When the modern killer AIDS first appeared in 1981, doctors had to try to solve a difficult and deadly puzzle. Lots of young, previously healthy people were dying of rare diseases. These diseases should have been completely harmless to humans – they were caused by germs or viruses that normally only affected birds, other animals or people who were already very sick from other diseases. After several years' research, scientists pinpointed the cause of the problem. It was a virus that we now call HIV (Human Immunodeficiency Virus). Inside the body, this virus slowly destroys a person's immune system – the part of them that fights disease. Once it has taken hold in a person's body, they develop full-blown AIDS (Acquired Immunodeficiency Syndrome). A person with AIDS has very little ability to fight off even the mildest of germs and viruses.

MONKEY PUZZLE

To this day, no one really knows where HIV came from. Some scientists think it was a monkey virus that suddenly changed its form and spread to humans. Others think it has always been on Earth, lying dormant for thousands of years. A few people have even suggested it was cooked up accidentally in a laboratory. So far, over 15 million people world-wide have been infected with HIV. Wherever this virus came from, doctors know they need to find a cure.

TRACKING A KILLER

You may not think of the flu as a big killer, but in 1918–19 an outbreak of an unusually nasty flu virus killed 25 million people. Causing 18 thousand deaths in London alone, it killed more people than the First World War itself. Aware that a strain (type) of the flu virus could turn nasty again, scientists keep a watchful eye on it. Each strain of the flu virus mutates (changes form) every season. Usually, it undergoes tiny changes called 'drifts' but sometimes it 'shifts', changing so dramatically that no one can fight it off. That's when the world has to worry. Scientists constantly monitor flu viruses. They are ready to sound the alarm if any of them undergo a large shift.

TRAVEL BUGS

It's not only people who enjoy the convenience of fast global travel – germs and viruses make the most of it too. Years ago, if a traveller picked up a deadly disease like yellow fever, they'd be seriously ill – or even dead – well before they reached their destination. This meant they were unlikely to spread the disease very far. These days, if you pick up something nasty, you could be in another continent before you have any symptoms. This means diseases can travel like wildfire around the globe. Health organisations around the world have to keep in close contact to let each other know of any big killers on the move.

RICH KILLER

In rich countries, many of us are worried about the way we eat and exercise. We know that diet and fitness can have a big effect on our health – they may even affect how long we live. Machines have replaced the need to do hard physical work – and as many of us have cars, we don't spend much time walking. Most of us have money to spend on fatty foods that contain very few vitamins. Our daily lives can be very stressful as we try to fit in everything we need to do. All these qualities of our modern lifestyle make us more likely than ever to suffer from diseases such as heart disease and cancer. These are the diseases that rich countries are interested in curing.

FOOD FOR THOUGHT

While rich countries spend billions of pounds researching high-tech cures for killers like heart disease, cancer and AIDS, a third of the world does not have even the most basic health care.

The World Health Organisation, a body of health experts from around the world, thinks we need to spend a minimum of £8 *on average* per person per year to give everyone on the planet the health care they need. People who are sick need more of this money than people who are well. *On average*, people in the UK are lucky enough to have over £700 spent on them. But in Nepal and the Sudan, the average spend per person is only 57 pence a year. Looking at these figures, it's not surprising that 8000 children die every day from the effects of a simple, preventable and treatable illness: diarrhoea.

Quiz

1 To make sure babies were born pretty, a French hospital in the 1660s
a) banned ugly doctors
b) banned loud noises
c) banned lemon juice

2 Lister dramatically reduced the numbers of people who died after surgery when he started using
a) electric lighting
b) disinfectants
c) spectacles

3 In the 1850s, a London doctor managed to stop an outbreak of cholera by removing
a) a pump handle
b) people's right to travel
c) a butcher's ear

4 Poor, sick people used to stand in stagnant pools because they were full of
a) bloodsucking grubs
b) healing moulds
c) warm water

5 People used to think that bad teeth were caused by
a) worms
b) tooth fairies
c) brushing them

6 People used to think they could protect themselves from the Plague by
a) drinking through a straw
b) sniffing flowers
c) touching the dead

7 To keep himself well, Benjamin Franklin used to spend up to an hour a day
a) horse riding
b) in the nude
c) kite flying

8 In the 1930s, the deadly disease typhoid was accidentally spread by a travelling
a) cook
b) salesman
c) doctor

9 Between 1918 and 1919, 25 million people died of
a) war wounds
b) the flu
c) the Plague

10 Tragically, every day, 8000 children die from the effects of
a) car accidents
b) diarrhoea
c) measles

Quiz Answers

CHAPTER 1 PAGE 29

1 - c,   2 - b,   3 - a *and* c (trick question),   4 - b,
5 - a,   6 - b,   7 - c,   8 - a,   9 - a,   10 - c

CHAPTER 2 PAGE 58

1 - c,   2 - a,   3 - a,   4 - c,   5 - b
6 - b,   7 - c,   8 - c   9 - a,   10 - b

CHAPTER 3 PAGE 74

1 - b,   2 - c,   3 - a,   4 - a,   5 - b,
6 - c,   7 - b,   8 - a,   9 - c,   10 - b

CHAPTER 4 PAGE 99

1 - a,   2 - b,   3 - b,   4 - b,   5 - a,
6 - b,   7 - c,   8 - a,   9 - c,   10 - b

CHAPTER 5 PAGE 133

1 - a,   2 - b,   3 - a,   4 - a,   5 - a,
6 - b,   7 - b,   8 - a,   9 - b,   10 - b

Index

acupuncture 50
AIDS 83, 94, 124, 128-129, 131
anaesthetics 10, 31, 35-36, 40-51, 109
antibiotics 76, 92-97, 108, 116
artificial organ 55

bath 60, 62, 77
blood 17, 28, 53-54, 107, 112
brain 9, 11, 50, 101, 118

cancer 35, 81-83, 131
cholera 60, 62, 121-122
clone 97-98
corpse 8-20, 66, 117

diabetes 114
drain 60, 62, 68, 122, 126-27

endoscope 36, 42

flu 94, 121, 130
freezing 20, 43-44, 91, 119-20

genetics 57, 97-98, 101-104
germs
    cleanliness and germs 60-61, 78
    disease and germs 65-73, 101, 113,
    121
    germ killers *see* antibiotics
spread of germs 121, 127, 130
glove 71-73
grave 19, 117, 122

heart
    heart beat 22, 101, 118
    heart disease 45, 83, 131
    heart surgery 53, 55
    theories about the heart 10, 17
holders down 44
Human Genome Project 103
hypnosis 50

Internet 20, 42

laser 34-35
leech 107

malaria 123
mould 76, 93
MRI scanner 27-28
mummy 9, 79, 119

operating theatre 15, 44, 60, 72-73

penicillin 76, 92-95
placebo 84
Plague 115-116, 122, 126
plant 43, 76-80, 83, 105
poison 51, 79, 82, 86
polio 91-92

quack 79, 83

radium 81-82
respirator 51, 101, 118

smallpox 76, 87-92
smoking 124-125
spa 77-78
spider's web 33
stethoscope 21-22
stone 109
surgery
    cleanliness and surgery 60, 68-71, 106
    early surgery 31-33, 109
    killing pain in surgery *see* anaesthetics
    modern surgery 34-36, 40, 106

toilet 60, 62, 64, 122, 127
tooth 15, 23, 47, 52, 60, 63, 113
transplant 53-56
tuberculosis 107
typhoid 60, 124, 126-127

ultrasound 26-27, 109
urine 68-69, 94, 113-114

vaccine 76, 86-92, 126
virus 84, 94, 101, 128-30

washing 66-69 *see also* bath

X-ray 8, 21, 23-26

If you have enjoyed this book, look out for:

THE SCIENCE MUSEUM
BOOK OF AMAZING FACTS

COMMUNICATION

Sarah Angliss

Get wired with a feast of weird and wonderful facts
about communications!
All the TV and radio ever broadcast is moving
continually through space.
Live pictures of Nelson Mandela's release from prison
in 1990 will soon be reaching Sirius, a star over
83 billion kilometres away.
The Internet is the descendant of a military secret
message-carrying system, designed to
survive a nuclear war.
Over 34 million computers are sold every year – but
when IBM first made them, they thought they'd be
lucky to sell more than five.

If you have enjoyed this book, look out for:

THE SCIENCE MUSEUM BOOK OF AMAZING FACTS

DISCOVERIES

Beverley Birch

For trailblazers – a feast of weird and wonderful facts
about discovery – old and new.
Rotting sugarbeet gave the first clues to the
causes of killer diseases.
A small girl playing in caves found Ice Age
paintings over 17,000 years old.
Radioactivity first revealed itself on a cloudy day
in Paris – in a desk drawer.
Peering into rainwater puddles, a curious
linen-draper discovered the invisible world of living
creatures that surrounds us.

If you have enjoyed this book, look out for:

THE SCIENCE MUSEUM BOOK OF AMAZING FACTS

INVENTIONS

Beverley Birch

For bright sparks – a feast of weird
and wonderful facts about inventions.
The inventors of the first robot were put
on trial for witchcraft.
In the 1700s, dead men's teeth, taken from skulls in
graveyards and battlefields, were used as false teeth.
The first electric light bulbs needed a health warning:
'Do not try and light with a match.'
The first working television was made
from a knitting needle, the lid of a hatbox,
an electric fan motor, and torch batteries, all put
together on top of an old tea-chest.

If you have enjoyed this book, look out for:

THE SCIENCE MUSEUM BOOK OF AMAZING FACTS

ENERGY

Anthony Wilson

Power up – a feast of weird and
wonderful facts about energy!
If your legs were as powerful as a flea's,
you'd be able to jump over an
80-storey skyscraper.
In 1986 two Japanese motorists
drove right across Australia without
using a single drop of fuel.
There's enough energy in one flash
of lightning to power all the lights in
a typical house for a year.
You can warm up a cup of coffee
just by stirring it.

SPORT

Colin M. Jarman

No sweat – a feast of weird and wonderful
facts about sport!
A modern tennis racket is so light that the
heaviest part is the glue holding it together.
Long jumpers can leap further at the equator than
they can at the Poles.
A squash ball hit at 240 kilometres per hour will
rebound off a wall at only 65 kilometres per hour ...

CONSTRUCTIONS

Chris Oxlade

For towering intellects – a feast of weird and
wonderful facts about constructions!
Mosquitoes brought the building of the
Panama Canal to a standstill.
The suspension cables of New York's Brooklyn Bridge
contain enough steel wire to stretch across the
Atlantic four times.
Tunnelling machines owe their design to the teredo
worm, which burrows through damp wood.
The Great Pyramid held the record for the world's
tallest building for nearly four thousand years.

If you have enjoyed this book, look out for:

THE SCIENCE MUSEUM BOOK OF AMAZING FACTS

EXPLORATION

Anthony Wilson

For far-out kids – a feast of weird
and wonderful facts about exploration!
People in ancient Peru thought that the
Earth was square.
Christopher Columbus kept a false log book
so that his men wouldn't find out how far
from home they really were.
In 1960, a balloon bigger than St Paul's Cathedral
was launched to study cosmic rays.
You can't have a boiled egg for breakfast
at the top of Mount Everest because boiling water
doesn't get hot enough.

If you have enjoyed this book, look out for:

THE SCIENCE MUSEUM BOOK OF AMAZING FACTS

TRANSPORT

Beverley Birch

For whizz kids – a feast of weird
and wonderful facts about transport!
The first air passengers were a sheep, a duck
and a cock, who sailed up in a hot air balloon,
watched by the King of France.
In 1838 the fastest journey across the Atlantic
(by steamship) took 15 days. Now *Concorde* can fly
the distance in 3 hours.
An American inventor has designed a bike with
54 speeds, 5 computers, a security system, a speech
synthesiser, a telephone, and a microfiche file.

ORDER FORM

Title	Author	ISBN	Price	
COMMUNICATIONS	Sarah Angliss	0 340 71475 1	3.99	☐
SPACE	Anthony Wilson	0 340 65696 4	3.99	☐
INVENTIONS	Beverley Birch	0 340 65697 2	3.99	☐
DISCOVERIES	Beverley Birch	0 340 68999 4	3.99	☐
CONSTRUCTIONS	Chris Oxlade	0 340 68994 3	3.99	☐
EXPLORATION	Anthony Wilson	0 340 69000 3	3.99	☐
TRANSPORT	Beverley Birch	0 340 65698 0	3.99	☐
ENERGY	Anthony Wilson	0 340 71477 8	3.99	☐
SPORT	Colin M. Jarman	0 340 71478 6	3.99	☐

All Hodder Children's Books are available at your local bookshop, or can be ordered direct from the publisher. Just tick the titles you would like and complete the details below. Prices and availability are subject to change without prior notice.

Please enclose a cheque or postal order made payable to *Bookpoint Limited*, and send to: Hodder Children's Books 39 Milton Park, Abingdon, OXON OX14 4TD, UK. Email Address: orders@bookpoint.co.uk

If you would prefer to pay by credit card, our call centre team would be delighted to take your order by telephone. Our direct line 01235 400414 (lines open 9.00 am - 6.00 pm Monday to Saturday, 24-hour message and answering service). Alternatively you can send a fax on *01235 400454*.

TITLE		FIRST NAME		SURNAME	
ADDRESS					
DAYTIME TEL:			POST CODE		

If you would prefer to pay by credit card, please complete:
Please debit my Visa/Access/Diner's Card/American Express (delete as applicable) card number:

Signature .... Expiry Date ....

If you would NOT like to receive further information on our products please tick the box. ☐